Maritime & Coastguard Agency

Wellbeing at Sea
A Pocket Guide for Seafarers

Connie S. Gehrt

Georgina Robinson

London: TSO

The beliefs, views and opinions expressed in this publication are those of the
authors and do not necessarily reflect the official policy or position of the
publisher or commissioning organisations.

Although the author and publisher have made every effort to ensure that
the information in this publication was correct at the time of press, neither
the author and/or the publisher assume and hereby disclaim any liability to
any party for any loss and/or damage, caused by errors and/or omissions,
whether such errors and/or omissions result from negligence, accident, and/
or any other cause. This publication is not intended as a substitute for the
medical advice of physicians. The reader should take independent medical
advice relating to his/her health with respect to any symptoms that may
require diagnosis or medical attention.

The publication may include hyperlinks to third-party content, advertising,
or websites, provided for the sake of convenience and interest.

The publishers do not endorse any advertising or products available from
external sources.

ISBN 978 0 11 553787 5

Printed in the United Kingdom for The Stationery Office
J003670826 C15 05/20

Contents

Preface   viii

Foreword   x

About the authors   xii

Introduction   xiv

| Section 1 General health and wellbeing | 1 |

1.1	**Diet**	**1**
1.1.1	Risks of being underweight or overweight	3
1.1.2	Special diets	7
1.1.3	Allergies	8
1.1.4	Intolerances	9
1.2	**Hydration**	**10**
1.3	**Seasickness**	**13**
1.4	**Personal hygiene**	**15**
1.4.1	How to wash your hands	17
1.4.2	How to brush your teeth and use dental floss	19
1.5	**Blood pressure and heart**	**21**
1.5.1	Blood pressure	21
1.5.2	Heart	22
1.6	**Tiredness and fatigue**	**23**
1.6.1	How to improve sleep onboard	26
1.7	**Managing climate conditions**	**26**
1.7.1	Sun	27

1.7.2	Heat exhaustion and heat stroke	29
1.7.3	Hypothermia	31
1.8	**Fitness and exercise**	**33**
1.9	**Musculoskeletal disorders (muscle and bone injuries)**	**34**
1.10	**Vibration and noise**	**36**
1.10.1	Vibration	37
1.10.2	Noise	39
1.11	**Infectious diseases**	**40**
1.12	**Sexuality**	**42**
1.12.1	Sexuality and the law	45
1.13	**Relationships**	**46**
1.13.1	Romantic relationships with other crew members	48
1.14	**Sex**	**49**
1.14.1	Consent	49
1.14.2	Avoiding unwanted pregnancy	52
1.14.3	Sexually transmitted diseases	56
1.15	**Pregnancy**	**58**
1.15.1	Managing pregnancy onboard	58
1.15.2	When your partner is pregnant	61

Section 2 Personal and social wellbeing
		63
2.1	**Communication**	**63**
2.1.1	Verbal and non-verbal communication	64
2.1.2	Teamwork	65
2.1.3	Conflict	66

2.2	Cultural differences	68
2.2.1	Gestures	68
2.3	Loneliness	72
2.3.1	Getting privacy	74
2.4	Bullying, harassment and discrimination	75
2.5	Crime	79
2.5.1	Theft	80
2.5.2	Piracy	81
2.5.3	Assault	83
2.5.4	Sexual assault and rape	84
2.5.5	Criminalisation	88
2.6	Whistle-blowing	89
2.7	Finance	91
2.8	Travel	94
2.9	Repatriation	100
2.10	Cyber security	102
2.10.1	Social media	104

Section 3 Mental and emotional wellbeing		**107**
3.1	Personal resilience	107
3.2	Work–life balance	109
3.3	Boredom	110
3.4	Smoking, alcohol and drugs	111
3.4.1	Smoking	111
3.4.2	Alcohol	113

3.4.3	Drugs	117
3.4.4	Addiction	124
3.5	**Overwork**	**125**
3.6	**Stress**	**127**
3.7	**Anxiety**	**130**
3.7.1	Generalised anxiety disorder	131
3.7.2	Post-traumatic stress disorder	134
3.7.3	Panic disorder	136
3.8	**Depression**	**139**
3.8.1	Symptoms of depression	140
3.8.2	Treatment for depression	141
3.9	**Self-harm and suicide**	**142**
3.9.1	Self-harm	142
3.9.2	Suicide	144
3.10	**Spiritual wellbeing**	**146**

Appendix		**149**
A.1	**Positive reflection**	**149**
A.2	**Relaxation techniques**	**149**
A.2.1	Breathing exercise	150
A.2.2	Mindfulness exercise	150
A.2.3	Body scan	151
A.2.4	Progressive relaxation	151
A.3	**Exercises to do onboard**	**152**
A.3.1	Warming up	153
A.3.2	The plank	154

A.3.3	The squat	155
A.3.4	Push-ups/press-ups	156
A.3.5	March in one place	157
A.3.6	The mountain climber	158
A.3.7	The double crunch	158
A.3.8	The reverse lunge	159
A.3.9	Cooling down	160
A.4	**Checking your body for illnesses**	**163**
A.4.1	Skin	163
A.4.2	Breasts	164
A.4.3	Testicles	166
A.4.4	Urine	166
A.4.5	Bowel health	167
A.4.6	Coughs	168
A.4.7	Hands and nails	168
A.5	**Useful contacts**	**169**
Index		173

Preface

Wellbeing is about you having a state of good health and fulfilment. It is not just the absence of illness, but also about achieving a positive mental state. Seafaring is a very demanding profession. Being far away from family and friends, being unable to leave the workplace and having fewer choices during non-working hours can affect your physical, mental and emotional health. With the average individual spending more than 90,000 hours in the workplace during their lives, the working environment can have a significant impact on wellbeing. And for seafarers, whilst onboard, the ship is not only your place of work but also your home.

Wellbeing initiatives from the company will have little effect unless you also take responsibility for your own wellbeing. This title contains practical advice and tips to help you monitor and improve your own and your fellow crew members' wellbeing. Written in simple English with illustrations and highlighted key facts, this book is an essential resource for all seafarers.

Acknowledgements from the authors

The authors fully acknowledge that this guidance builds on many different sources and experiences. Where relevant or particularly useful, sources are provided in references. We acknowledge that there may be sources that are not specifically mentioned or referenced because of lack of awareness, documentation or simply human frailty. We would, however, like to acknowledge and thank all those that participate in expanding the knowledge in this area and those that may also directly or indirectly have influenced this book.

Acknowledgement from MCA

This title would not have been possible without the advice and support of the following people and organisations:

Reverend Ijeoma Ajibade, The Mission to Seafarers

David Appleton, Nautilus International

Mark Carden, National Union of Rail, Maritime and Transport Workers

Tom Holmer, ISWAN

Dr Pierfrancesco Lepore, MSC Cruise Management UK Ltd

Reverend Canon Ken Peters, former Director of Justice and Public Affairs, Mission to Seafarers

Tim Springett, UK Chamber of Shipping

Caitlin Vaughan, ISWAN

Foreword

So much of our industry is driven by processes and targets that it is easy to forget about the most integral part – the people. Meaning and self-fulfilment are fundamental to the human experience. Work becomes meaningful when it serves a purpose that aligns with the needs and beliefs of the individual, allowing them to develop and thrive. We all know that when work is meaningful, it is more enjoyable, we have more motivation and we act with more thought and care.

Recently, I feel that there has been a perceptible shift in working culture to reflect this. Employers increasingly acknowledge that they have a duty of care towards their staff that extends beyond the processes and policies that keep them safe. More than ever, we understand that in order for organisations to succeed, we must enable individuals to engage with work in a way that fulfils their intellectual, emotional and psychological needs, as well as their physical needs, both inside and outside of work. Wellbeing encompasses this feeling of fulfilment in every aspect of life.

We are increasingly aware that life onboard can take a toll on the health and wellbeing of seafarers, which in turn can have an impact on the health of the organisation through reduced productivity, increased turnover and more accidents. Consequently, the maritime industry must think about how to maintain healthy, contented and engaged seafarers. The Maritime & Coastguard Agency is committed to the vision of 'Safer Lives, Safer Ships, Cleaner Seas'. We know from a wealth of experience that wellbeing is a critical and often overlooked part of safety. The best organisations take a proactive approach to wellbeing; they actively strive for commitment and collaboration from every part of the organisation – from top management through to the workforce.

Recognising this, the MCA, with the support of our social partners and other like-minded stakeholders, have created two complementary publications, *Wellbeing at Sea: A Guide for Organisations* and *Wellbeing at Sea: A Pocket Guide for Seafarers*, with the aim of inspiring and supporting companies and individuals to make wellbeing a priority onboard. Using their knowledge of the industry, the authors provide tailored and pragmatic advice that will enable companies and seafarers to build resilience and engender a culture of safety and wellbeing onboard.

These two companion books are an essential read for companies that understand that in order to be productive and safe, seafarers must also be well.

Brian Johnson
Chief Executive
Maritime & Coastguard Agency

About the authors

Connie S. Gehrt

Connie S. Gehrt has a long experience with occupational health and safety at sea and has been working in the maritime industry since 2002.

Connie is the managing director and owner of the consultancy company CONOVAH – Health and Safety Solutions, which, among others, provides consultancy and training worldwide on wellbeing, stress management, suicide prevention, bullying and harassment, leadership, ship–shore communication and safety, and provides global psychological crisis counselling. She has been doing a study on loneliness at sea and she provides leadership and business coaching. She is also a counsellor at the Danish Suicide Prevention Lifeline.

From 2007 to 2017 Connie was the managing director of SEAHEALTH, Denmark. During her management SEAHEALTH developed to be a worldwide recognised organisation for providing important tools and guidelines for the industry. Before that Connie worked as a special advisor and chief counsellor for the Danish Maritime Authority.

She has a master's degree in law from University of Copenhagen and a master's degree in the psychology of organisations from Roskilde University. She also has coaching and leadership education from DISPUK.

Georgina Robinson

Georgina Robinson is currently working as a CBT therapist. She works in therapeutic environments assessing mental illness, managing risk in terms of suicidal thoughts, self-harm as well as delivering interventions to individuals with depression, general anxiety disorder, panic disorder, phobias and other associated disorders, including anger management.

She has a strong research background. Her interests are in the behavioural and psychological aspects of pain management, analgesic use in painful conditions, as well as developing and evaluating interventions in self-management of pain. Her work within seafaring has included developing and evaluating mental and physical health interventions for seafarers at sea.

Introduction

Seafaring can be an exciting and rewarding job, but it can also challenge your mental, physical and emotional endurance. Wellbeing is an important part of keeping yourself healthy and happy onboard.

Wellbeing isn't just about your physical health; it's about your social, emotional and mental health too. Wellbeing means you'll cope well with challenges, feel good about yourself, and be able to form and maintain meaningful relationships. In short, wellbeing affects everything you do in your day-to-day life.

If you feel like your wellbeing is suffering, talking to a loved one or a professional can help. Your company may provide some contacts for you, and you'll find others at the back of this book. When you're at sea, being able to spot threats to your wellbeing will put you in control of your health and let you catch problems before they become serious.

This pocketbook contains easy-to-read information on a range of wellbeing issues and includes practical ways to manage your wellbeing while you're onboard.

Structure of the book

This book is split into four sections:

1) General health and wellbeing
2) Personal and social wellbeing
3) Mental and emotional wellbeing
4) Appendix, including tips for relaxation, exercise and general health.

The headings within each section contain features (see image below) to help you spot and manage wellbeing issues.

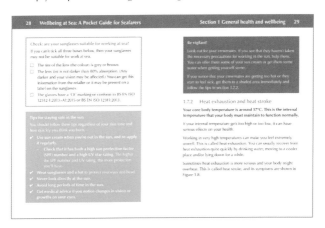

1 General health and wellbeing

1.1 Diet

Controlling your diet onboard a vessel might be difficult because you have a limited choice of food.

The quality and amount of food that you have onboard will depend on the company that you work for, but you can still make good choices with what you're given.

A balanced diet gives your body all the vitamins and nutrients it needs.

Vitamins and nutrients are substances that help your body to function normally. Table 1.1 and Figure 1.1 show the recommended daily intake of different foods for an adult.

Aside from having a balanced diet, it's also important to be aware of calories.

Calories are the amount of energy in an item of food or drink.

The average adult needs 2000–2500 calories per day to maintain a healthy body weight. You may need more or less than this, depending on how active you are.

You should get all the calories that you need from a healthy and balanced diet.

There are many fitness and diet apps you can use to work out how many calories you need per day. You can also use these apps to find out how many calories you are getting from different foods.

Table 1.1 The proportions of foods that adults are recommended to eat each day

Food group	Proportion of total calories (per day)	Healthy examples	Examples that are less healthy or unhealthy
Fruit and vegetables	40% (try to eat 5 portions of fruit and/or vegetables per day)	Any fresh fruit or vegetable	Fruit juice or smoothies
Carbohydrates	38%	High-fibre, wholegrain varieties of pasta, bread or other grains	White bread Normal pasta
Proteins	12%	Beans, pulses, fish, eggs and white meat	Processed meats such as bacon, ham and sausages
Dairy (and alternatives)	8%	Low-fat and low-sugar milk, cheese and yogurt	Flavoured yogurts, full-fat milk

Food group	Proportion of total calories (per day)	Healthy examples	Examples that are less healthy or unhealthy
Fats	1%	Unsaturated fats; vegetable, rapeseed, olive and sunflower oils	Condiments such as ketchup. Biscuits, sweets, cakes, crisps, chocolate and ice cream

1.1.1   Risks of being underweight or overweight

Eating too little or having a diet that is low in vitamins and nutrients can lead you to become underweight.

Being underweight can cause you to have:

* Brittle bones that break easily
* A weak immune system, so you get ill more often and recover slowly
* Fertility issues.

The food you eat will affect how much energy you have during the day.

Eating too much or eating a lot of sugary or fatty foods can lead to your becoming overweight.

Figure 1.1 A balanced diet. Source: Crown copyright.
Public Health England in association with the Welsh
Government, Food Standards Scotland and the Food Standards
Agency in Northern Ireland.

Figure 1.2 shows some of the risks associated with being overweight.

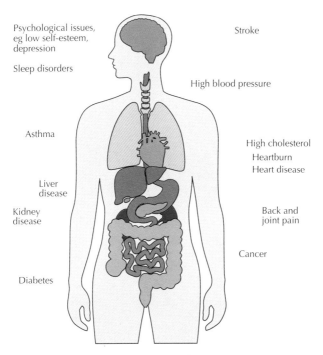

Figure 1.2 The risks of being overweight

Check your body mass index

Calculating your body mass index (BMI) can show you if you might be overweight. Be aware that BMI might not be accurate for everyone. You should just use it as a general guide to help you achieve a healthy lifestyle.

1) To calculate your BMI, divide your weight in kilograms by your height in metres, and then divide the answer by your height in metres again.

For example: Weight = 70 kg, Height = 1.75 m
Calculation: 70/1.75 = 40, then 40/1.75 = BMI of 22.9

For most adults, a BMI of:

- 18.5 means you're underweight
- 18.5 to 24.9 means you're a healthy weight
- 25 to 29.9 means you're overweight
- 30 to 39.9 means you're obese
- 40 or above means you're severely obese.

Note: if you're very muscular, you might have a high BMI, so check your waist circumference too.

2) You can use a measuring tape to measure your waist. Men with a waist measurement of 94 cm or more, and women with a waist measurement of 80 cm or more, are at risk of developing obesity-related health problems.

Tips for improving your diet

✔ **Download a healthy-eating app** to help you monitor what you eat.

✔ **Aim to drink 2 litres of water a day** (read more in section 1.2).

✔ **Don't deprive yourself of treats.** Just control your portion sizes.

✔ **Don't skip important meals** like breakfast.

✔ **Try to keep a balanced diet.** Eat more fruit and vegetables when you have a chance.

✔ **Avoid adding salt or other condiments to your food.** A lot of the food you eat at sea will be canned. Canned foods contain a lot of salt already, so try to avoid adding more, because this can raise your blood pressure. (See section 1.5 for information on blood pressure.)

1.1.2   Special diets

Some people have a restricted or controlled diet for moral, medical or religious reasons. Be sensitive about your crewmates' choices.

If you have a special diet, you should inform the master, the company and the cooks onboard, so they can make the necessary arrangements.

You have the right to have access to food that meets your religious or cultural needs. This is covered in Maritime Labour Convention (MLC) regulation 3.2.

1.1.3   Allergies

Allergic reactions happen when your immune system incorrectly starts attacking something that you've eaten, inhaled or touched, thinking that it's a threat to your body.

This response can be immediate or it can happen up to 24 hours later. Table 1.2 lists some common reactions.

Table 1.2 Symptoms of mild and severe allergic reactions

Mild reaction	Severe reaction
• Hives (itchy red spots on skin) • Itching • Blocked nose • Rash • Itchy throat • Watery or itchy eyes	• Stomach cramps or pain • Diarrhoea • Pain/tightness in chest • Difficulty breathing • Heart palpitations • Swelling of face, throat, tongue • Unconsciousness

If your body has this reaction to anything, then you may be allergic to it.

The simplest way to manage an allergy is to avoid the thing that's causing a reaction.

The symptoms of allergic reactions can be treated using medications called antihistamines.

Tips for managing allergies at sea

✔ **Make sure your company, your medical examiner and your medical provider onboard know what you're allergic to and how severe your reactions are.** This will help them put procedures in place to manage your allergies onboard.

✔ **Bring enough medication to manage your symptoms.**

   – **Pack enough medication to last your entire contract,** in case it isn't available anywhere else.

   – **Take the medication with you regardless of how likely it is that you will have a reaction.**

✔ **If you know a crewmate is allergic to something, try your best to keep it away from them.**

   – Wash yourself and your hands regularly to stop cross-contamination (where you transfer the allergen from one place to another by accident).

✔ **Let caterers know if you are allergic to any food.** They might be able to put procedures in place to make sure you're not served anything that you're allergic to.

1.1.4   Intolerances

Food intolerances do not involve the immune system. They occur when your body finds it difficult to digest something that you've consumed.

Food intolerances are not life-threatening.

Symptoms of food intolerance include stomach pain or cramps, bloating, wind, diarrhoea, skin rashes or itching. These symptoms usually happen a few hours after you've had the food that you're intolerant to.

If you have these symptoms, it can be difficult to identify what caused them. See the tips below to find out how you can identify a food intolerance.

> **Tips for identifying a food intolerance**
>
> ✔ **Keep a food diary.** Note down everything you eat, along with any reactions and when these occur. This will help you narrow down the foods you might be intolerant to.
>
> ✔ **Cut out foods that you suspect you might be intolerant to.** You can slowly reintroduce these foods into your diet in different amounts to see if they have any effect. Note down the amount of each food you eat, if or when symptoms occur, and how severe they are. This will help you identify the intolerance and show you how much of the food you can eat safely.

1.2   Hydration

Water helps your body perform many important functions, such as absorbing nutrients, digesting food, regulating temperature and removing waste. It also helps you to focus.

You should drink about 2 litres of water a day.

Working in hot temperatures, being ill, drinking alcohol, hard physical work and injuries such as burns can cause dehydration. Figure 1.3 shows how dehydration affects the body.

Dehydration is when your body loses too much water.

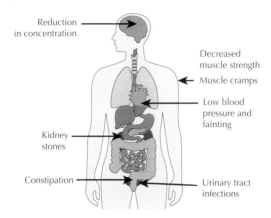

Figure 1.3 The effects of dehydration

Check: are you dehydrated?

If you have one or more of these symptoms, you might be dehydrated:

☐ Increased thirst

☐ Reduced urination

☐ Dark urine (healthy urine is the colour of pale straw)

☐ Tiredness

☐ Headaches

List continues on next page

Are you dehydrated? *Continued*

- ☐ Dizziness
- ☐ Weakness
- ☐ Palpitations (your heartbeat feels like it's jumping or irregular)
- ☐ Dry skin

Be vigilant!

Dehydration can have serious effects on the mind and body. You should look after yourself and your crewmates, checking for any signs of dehydration. Make sure you're all drinking water regularly, especially when exercising or working in hot conditions.

If a crew member shows any of the signs below, get medical help immediately.

- Temperature higher than 39°C (103°F) that doesn't settle with temperature-lowering measures and medication
- Confusion
- Lethargy
- Continued headaches
- Seizures
- Difficulty breathing
- Chest pains
- Fainting
- No urine in the last 12 hours

Tips for staying hydrated

✔ Aim to drink 2 litres of water a day. (Drink more when working in hot environments.)

✔ Drink a glass of water as soon as you wake up.

✔ Replace caffeinated and fizzy drinks with water.

✔ Make sure you can access drinking water easily around the vessel.

✔ If you're exercising, or working in a hot environment, stop to drink some water every 10–15 minutes.

✔ Keep a check on the colour of your urine; it should be light in colour and shouldn't smell.

1.3   Seasickness

Seasickness can affect anyone on the sea at any time. This means that even experienced seafarers can get seasick.

Seasickness is a type of motion sickness. It's caused by repetitive movement that confuses the parts of the body responsible for balance and steadiness.

Most of the time, you can just remove yourself from a situation that's making you sick, but this isn't always possible onboard. So, it's always a good idea to take travel sickness medication with you. This can help to relieve some of the symptoms.

Seasickness tablets should also be available in the medical chest onboard.

Check: are you seasick?

Any one of these symptoms can indicate seasickness:

- ☐ Excessive sweating
- ☐ Dizziness
- ☐ Headaches
- ☐ Fatigue
- ☐ Nausea
- ☐ Vomiting.

Normally, you should be able to overcome these symptoms after a few days of getting used to the ship or after using travel sickness medication.

If you feel seasick on and off the vessel, or your symptoms continue after taking medication, get medical help as soon as possible. Contact the medical provider onboard. If you don't have access to a medical provider onboard, you may need to contact the Telemedical Advice Service (TMAS) or seek shore-side help.

Tips for managing seasickness

✔ **Take medication for travel sickness.** Be sure to check the instructions and side-effects, as some medications can make you drowsy and affect your safety at work.

✔ **Have a ginger biscuit or drink some ginger tea.** Ginger can help you feel less nauseous.

✔ **Walk to the middle of the vessel, if possible.** There is less motion there than in other parts of the boat.

✔ **Get some fresh air.** Being in small spaces, like cabins and engine rooms, might make you feel worse.

✔ **Avoid looking at screens.** Look at something stationary on the horizon instead.

✔ **Don't eat heavy meals or drink alcohol before you go onboard.**

✔ **Stay hydrated.** Keep sipping cool water. Vomiting can lead to dehydration.

1.4   Personal hygiene

Seafarers live and work together in close quarters. This means that it's easier for infectious diseases to spread (see section 1.11).

With good hygiene (including regular washing of hands), the risk of infection will remain low.

Tips for good personal hygiene

Body:

✔ **Wash your hands regularly, especially after using the toilet.** See section 1.4.1 on how you should wash your hands.

✔ **Wash your body and hair with soap at least once a day.**

✔ **Men should always wash under the foreskin** (if not circumcised) using soap and water.

✔ **Women should change sanitary towels regularly and dispose of them in sanitary bins or in an incinerator.**

✔ **Brush your teeth after each meal, and floss or use interdental brushes daily.** See section 1.4.2 on how you should brush your teeth and use dental floss.

✔ **Replace your toothbrush regularly.**

Clothing:

✔ **Change into clean clothes daily.**

✔ **Make sure that you wash your clothes regularly – especially underwear,** which should be washed after one use.

✔ **Make sure that you wear footwear in shared spaces, especially bathrooms.** You can wear shower shoes while using shared showers.

✔ **Don't put footwear on surfaces where you eat or sleep,** eg bed, canteen tables.

✔ **Store dirty clothes away from clean clothes.** Use a laundry bin to collect dirty clothes between washes.

Other:

✔ **When you sneeze or cough, do it into a tissue** (or, if tissues aren't available, the inside of your elbow) to stop the spread of infection when you touch things with your hands.

✔ **Throw used tissues in the bin.**

✔ If you're suffering from vomiting and/or diarrhoea, limit contact with colleagues until you've been **symptom-free for 48 hours.**

✔ **Wash towels often** (at least once a week) and don't share them with others.

✔ **Cover cuts and wounds with plasters or other appropriate medical barriers.**

1.4.1   How to wash your hands

You use your hands while you work, when you interact with others, when you eat or prepare food, and when you wash yourself.

This means that the hands encounter more pathogens (tiny organisms that cause disease) than any other part of our body, and infection can easily spread.

Rinsing your hands isn't enough. Pathogens can build up in hard-to-reach places (eg under your nails and in the gaps between your fingers).

Figure 1.4 shows how to wash your hands:

1) Wet your hands with clean running water, then apply soap.

2) Rub your hands together to lather the soap.

3 & 4) Scrub the soap around your hands, making sure you get under the nails and cover the palms and backs of your hands. This should take at least 20 seconds.

5) Rinse your hands with running water to wash the soap off.

6) Dry your hands with a clean, dry towel or dryer.

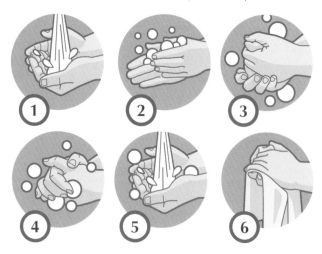

Figure 1.4 How to wash your hands

1.4.2   How to brush your teeth and use dental floss

When you eat or drink something, any residue that is left in your mouth feeds harmful bacteria that can cause tooth decay.

Brushing and using dental floss gets rid of or reduces the amount of these bacteria, keeping your teeth and gums healthy.

Getting dental care while at sea can be difficult, so it's very important that you look after your teeth to avoid infections and disease.

You should brush your teeth at least twice a day as shown in Figure 1.5: once in the morning before you've eaten, and once after all your meals for the day.

If you don't have time to brush after every meal, you can chew some sugar-free gum. But don't rely just on this. Brushing is still the best way to keep your teeth clean and healthy.

Brush:

1) Put a small amount of toothpaste (approximately the size of a pea) on a clean brush.
2) Brush the outer, inner and side surfaces of each tooth with the bristles, using a gentle back-and-forth motion. The process should take about 2 minutes for the whole of the mouth.
3) Finish by gently brushing your tongue and gums.

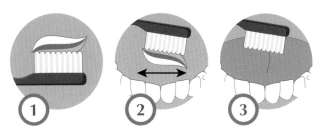

Figure 1.5 How to brush your teeth

Use dental floss, interdental brushes or sticks as shown in Figure 1.6 and repeat the process for every tooth:

1) Cut a length of dental floss and wrap each end around an index or middle finger, so you have a firm grip.

2) Use your thumbs to wiggle the length of floss (or interdental brush) slowly down the gap between two teeth.

3) Scrape the floss gently up the length of the tooth.

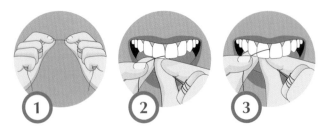

Figure 1.6 How to floss your teeth

1.5   Blood pressure and heart

1.5.1   Blood pressure

Blood pressure is the force that keeps the blood pumping around your body.

Your blood carries oxygen and nutrients around the body to maintain life.

A lot of factors can affect your blood pressure, but the ones that you can control include diet, exercise and smoking.

Smoking and eating unhealthy foods can increase blood pressure by causing your blood vessels to become narrower.

Blood pressure can be too high or too low.

High blood pressure can put a strain on and cause damage to your blood vessels and major organs such as the heart, brain and kidneys.

Low blood pressure can make you feel sick, confused, dizzy and weak. It can also make you faint. Low blood pressure can become very serious if it means that your body isn't getting the oxygen it needs.

You should have had a blood-pressure check during your medical examination.

1.5.2   Heart

Your heart is about the size of your fist. It's responsible for pumping blood around the body, providing nutrients and oxygen and removing waste.

Your diet and lifestyle can affect how well your heart works. Exercise and a healthy diet are better for your heart than an unhealthy lifestyle.

Other things that can have a negative effect on the heart include stress, which can lead to heart disease. Figure 1.7 shows some of the symptoms of heart disease.

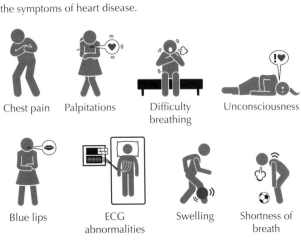

| Chest pain | Palpitations | Difficulty breathing | Unconsciousness |

| Blue lips | ECG abnormalities | Swelling | Shortness of breath |

Figure 1.7 Symptoms of heart disease

Tips for a healthy heart

✔ **Exercise regularly.** See section 1.8 to find out how you can exercise onboard.

✔ **Maintain a healthy BMI.** See section 1.1 to find out how to calculate your BMI.

✔ **Maintain a healthy diet.** See section 1.1 to find out how to improve your diet.

✔ **Don't smoke.** See section 3.4 to find out how to stop.

✔ **Cut down alcohol use.** See section 3.4 to find out how.

✔ **Try to manage your stress.** See the relaxation techniques in section A.2 of the appendix for help.

1.6 Tiredness and fatigue

Long working hours, irregular shift patterns and short turnarounds in port can lead to tiredness and fatigue.

Be vigilant!

Your crewmates might not realise that they're tired or fatigued, or they might try to work through it. Make sure you look out for signs of tiredness and fatigue in crew members.

If you think a crew member may be putting themselves and others at risk because of fatigue or tiredness, you should speak to your manager.

You should also speak to your colleague and help them manage their fatigue using the tips in this section.

Tiredness is when you have energy but feel weak or heavy. You can usually recover quickly from tiredness with rest.

Fatigue is a state of physical and mental exhaustion. It can build up over time and is hard to recover from.

Fatigue can be caused by lack of sleep, poor-quality sleep, jet lag, stress, boredom, poor diet, using drugs or alcohol, shift work, high workload, constant background noise and vibration.

Tiredness and fatigue can have a big effect on your safety and the safety of the people you work with.

Tips for managing fatigue
- ✔ **Make sure that you know and keep to the minimum hours of rest and the maximum hours of work.** For more information, look at MLC 2006 and the International Maritime Organization's (IMO) guidelines on fatigue.
- ✔ **Try to improve the quality of your sleep** (see section 1.6.1).
- ✔ **If you don't have time to sleep or rest properly, have a 10- to 20-minute nap.**
- ✔ Unhealthy food can make you feel sluggish, so try to **make healthy eating choices**. Food that's high in protein can increase energy.
- ✔ **Use caffeine to increase alertness** but don't use it if you're fighting to stay awake, as it can trick your body into using more energy than you have.
- ✔ Drink a cup of coffee before a nap. Caffeine takes about 20 minutes to have an effect, so it will start to benefit you when you wake up from your short nap.
- ✔ **Drink plenty of water.**
- ✔ **Try a short period of exercise** (see section A.3 of the appendix).

Check: are you fatigued?

If you have one or more of these symptoms, you might be fatigued:

- ☐ Shortness of breath
- ☐ Muscle weakness/pain
- ☐ Easily tired
- ☐ Lack of motivation
- ☐ Difficulty concentrating
- ☐ Difficulty making decisions
- ☐ Poor memory
- ☐ Poor coordination
- ☐ Don't feel refreshed by sleep
- ☐ Headache
- ☐ Feeling nauseous
- ☐ Feeling low in mood
- ☐ Falling asleep suddenly and without meaning to
- ☐ Loss of appetite
- ☐ Palpitations (jumping, irregular heartbeat)
- ☐ Irritable/mood swings

Note: fatigue can be serious. If you feel that your fatigue is affecting the safety of the crew, report it immediately.

If your fatigue doesn't improve after rest, seek medical advice.

1.6.1   How to improve sleep onboard

If you find it difficult to get the sleep you need, some small changes can make a big difference.

Here are some things you should and shouldn't do before going to sleep:

DO:	DON'T
• Block out as much noise and light as possible by using an eye mask, headphones or ear plugs. • Make sure your bed is clean and comfortable. • Make sure you're a comfortable temperature in bed, not too hot or too cold. • Eat a balanced diet.	• Work while you're in bed. • Smoke or use any other stimulants, like caffeine, just before going to bed. • Use your phone or any other devices in bed. • Do intense exercise just before bedtime. • Go to bed if you're not tired. • Drink alcohol close to bedtime. It can stop you from getting deep sleep.

1.7   Managing climate conditions

As a seafarer, you may travel to lots of different places with different climates. It's important that you're aware of how some of these conditions can affect your health.

1.7.1 Sun

The sun releases a type of energy called ultraviolet (UV) radiation.

You encounter this radiation naturally during the day, but lots of factors (amount of shade, altitude, etc.) can affect how much of it you're exposed to.

Being at sea can mean that you're exposed to much more sunlight and UV radiation. It can be increased by the reflection of light from the sea and in areas of ice.

Being exposed to the sun comes with benefits as well as risks. You can see some of these in Table 1.3.

Table 1.3 Benefits and risks of exposure to sunlight

Benefits	Risks
• Exposure to UV radiation produces vitamin D, which is essential for healthy bones, teeth and muscles. • Being in the sun can improve your mood.	• Sunburn on the skin and in the eyes • Blindness • Skin cancer (see section A.4 of the appendix to learn how to check for skin cancer).

Check: are your sunglasses suitable for working at sea?

If you can't tick all three boxes below, then your sunglasses may not be suitable for work at sea.

- ☐ The tint of the lens (the colour) is grey or brown.
- ☐ The lens tint is not darker than 80% absorption. (Any darker and your vision may be affected.) You can get this information from the retailer or it may be present on a label on the sunglasses.
- ☐ The glasses have a 'CE' marking or conform to BS EN ISO 12312-1:2013+A1:2015 or BS EN ISO 12311:2013.

Tips for staying safe in the sun

You should follow these tips regardless of your skin tone and how quickly you think you burn.

- ✔ Use sun cream when you're out in the sun, and re-apply it regularly.
    - Check that it has both a high sun protection factor (SPF) number and a high UV star rating. The higher the SPF number and UV rating, the more protection you'll have.
- ✔ Wear sunglasses and a hat to protect your eyes and head.
- ✔ Never look directly at the sun.
- ✔ Avoid long periods of time in the sun.
- ✔ Get medical advice if you notice changes in vision or growths on your eyes.

Be vigilant!

Look out for your crewmates. If you see that they haven't taken the necessary precautions for working in the sun, help them. You can offer them some of your sun cream or get them some water when getting yourself some.

If you notice that your crewmates are getting too hot or they start to feel sick, get them to a shaded area immediately and follow the tips in section 1.7.2.

1.7.2   Heat exhaustion and heat stroke

Your core body temperature is around 37°C. This is the internal temperature that your body must maintain to function normally.

If your internal temperature gets too high or too low, it can have serious effects on your health.

Working in very high temperatures can make you feel extremely unwell. This is called heat exhaustion. You can usually recover from heat exhaustion quite quickly by drinking water, moving to a cooler place and/or lying down for a while.

Sometimes heat exhaustion is more serious and your body might overheat. This is called heat stroke, and its symptoms are shown in Figure 1.8.

Figure 1.8 Symptoms of heat stroke

Heat stroke can be fatal. You should ask for help immediately if you suspect you, or a crewmate, are suffering from it.

You can help someone suffering from heat stroke by removing some of their clothing and placing ice packs or wet towels on their head, armpits, groin and neck.

Tips for avoiding heat exhaustion

- ✔ **Stay hydrated.** You might need to drink more water than normal in high temperatures.
- ✔ **Take breaks in cooler areas** if you work in high-temperature areas for long periods of time.
- ✔ **Wear comfortable, lightweight clothes.**
- ✔ **Wear light-coloured clothing.** Black and other dark colours absorb heat.

1.7.3   Hypothermia

Hypothermia is when your core body temperature drops below 35°C. This happens when you're exposed to cold conditions.

You can get hypothermia by:

- Falling overboard
- Wearing damp clothes
- Wearing clothes that don't keep you warm
- Excessive use of drugs/alcohol
- Being exposed to low temperatures
- Being exposed to extremely windy conditions when temperatures are low.

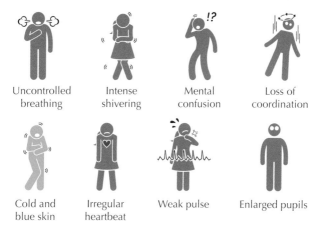

| Uncontrolled breathing | Intense shivering | Mental confusion | Loss of coordination |

| Cold and blue skin | Irregular heartbeat | Weak pulse | Enlarged pupils |

Figure 1.9 Symptoms of hypothermia

Hypothermia can be fatal, so if you suspect that you or a crewmate have it (see Figure 1.9 for the symptoms), get help immediately.

The box below shows some things that you should and shouldn't do while you wait for help.

DO:	DON'T
• Move the person to a warmer room/indoors.	• Put them in a hot bath.
• Remove any wet clothes and dry them.	• Use heat lamps to warm them up.
• Wrap them in blankets.	• Massage their limbs.
• Give them something warm to drink and something sugary to eat if they can manage it.	• Give them alcohol.

Be vigilant!

If you're helping a crewmate who you think is hypothermic, be careful. Don't try to warm them up quickly, because this can be dangerous for their health. Follow the tips below.

Tips for avoiding hypothermia

✔ **Wear warm clothes**. Wear layers of clothing, so that you can add clothes or remove them when you get too cold or too hot.

✔ **Avoid alcohol.** Drink warm non-alcoholic drinks.

✔ **Change out of wet clothes as soon as possible.** Wear waterproof layers if you can't change clothes often.

1.8   Fitness and exercise

Exercising onboard can be difficult for a seafarer because of long working hours, limited space and lack of equipment. But it's important to make some time for it.

Just 15–20 minutes of exercise, three times a week, can have a big effect on your mind and body.

Exercise has many health benefits. It can help you build muscle, maintain or lose weight, and increase stamina. It can also improve your mood.

Regular exercise can reduce your risk of developing heart disease, stroke, diabetes, cancer and dementia.

Tips for keeping fit

✔ You can find examples of exercises you can easily do onboard in section A.3 of the appendix.

✔ **Plan and set a goal.** What do you want to achieve and how will you do this?

✔ **Look for opportunities** to exercise. A spare 20 minutes is all you need.

✔ **Reward success.** Make a note of how you're going to reward yourself if you achieve a goal.

✔ **Keep a record of your workouts.** What did you do and what did you achieve?

✔ **Think about how you can make exercise more fun.** Will listening to music or asking colleagues if they want to join in make exercise more fun?

✔ **Try to exercise regularly,** so it becomes a habit. Set aside some time in your schedule each day just for exercise.

✔ Don't worry if you miss a few days; just make sure you start again.

1.9 Musculoskeletal disorders (muscle and bone injuries)

Musculoskeletal disorders (MSDs) are injuries or disorders that affect your bones and muscles.

MSDs tend to affect your movement (see Figure 1.10 for the parts of the body affected). They include muscle pain/tears/damage, varicose veins, arthritis, stress fractures, bone breaks and repetitive strain injuries.

General symptoms of MSDs include:

- Aches and pain
- Stiff joints
- Swelling
- Muscle weakness.

You need to be aware of MSDs, as your work may put you at extra risk of developing them.

The risk of developing MSDs increases if your tasks are:

- Repetitive
- Involve a lot of physical exertion, eg pushing/pulling loads
- Involve repetitive or continual awkward movement.

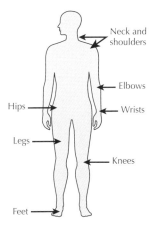

Figure 1.10 Areas commonly affected by MSDs

Not having enough time to recover after or between tasks can also increase the risk of developing an MSD.

> **Tips for avoiding MSDs**
>
> ✔ **Practise safe manual handling procedures.** Make sure you follow company policy and training. You can also find further guidance on manual handling in the *Code of Safe Working Practices for Merchant Seafarers* (COSWP) and at http://www.hse.gov.uk/pubns/indg143.pdf
>
> ✔ **Maintain a healthy diet and exercise.** Physical fitness lowers your risk of developing MSDs. See sections 1.1 and 1.8.
>
> ✔ **Rest.** Resting your body is important for recovery.
>
> ✔ **Get physiotherapy.** Physiotherapists can give you advice, information and therapy to help with your MSD. You can get more information and/or a referral from your doctor.

1.10   Vibration and noise

Noise and vibration are two of the main hazards that a seafarer is exposed to. Common sources of noise and vibration onboard include engines, machinery, equipment and the vessel itself.

Being onboard a vessel means that you might be exposed to much higher levels of noise and vibration than you normally would be onshore.

Being surrounded by high levels of vibration and noise can have a significant impact on your health.

1.10.1 Vibration

There are two main types of vibration: whole-body vibration (see Figure 1.11) and hand–arm vibration (see Figure 1.12).

Vessels vibrate as they navigate through choppy waters, and also due to vibrating machinery onboard. Poor vessel design can increase vibration.

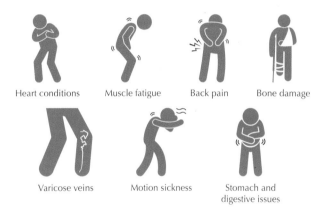

Heart conditions   Muscle fatigue   Back pain   Bone damage

Varicose veins   Motion sickness   Stomach and digestive issues

Figure 1.11 Effects of whole-body vibration

Hand–arm vibration is caused by using machinery, eg a chipping machine or handheld grinder.

These types of vibration can cause damage to the body. The amount and type of damage done depends on the amount of time you've been exposed to the vibration and the size and speed of the vibration.

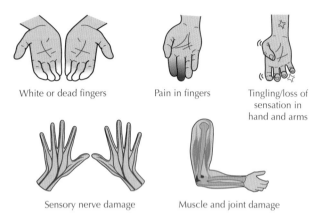

White or dead fingers   Pain in fingers   Tingling/loss of
sensation in
hand and arms

Sensory nerve damage   Muscle and joint damage

Figure 1.12 Effects of hand–arm vibration

Tips for working with vibration

✔ Always wear the correct PPE: sturdy boots, shock
absorbers, etc.

✔ Check company risk assessments referring to vibration.

✔ Check how much time you should be spending around
equipment that causes vibration and noise. This should
be in the risk assessment or company policy.

✔ Recognise the signs of whole-body vibration and hand–
arm vibration. Seek medical help quickly.

✔ If you believe that there is a serious problem with vibration
onboard, you should report it to your company
immediately. They may be able to do something about it.

1.10.2 Noise

The vessel can be a noisy working environment.

Working in loud or consistently noisy areas can lead to sleep disturbance, hearing loss, high blood pressure and heart disease.

Sudden loud noises can also cause damage to your hearing.

Ideally, you should only work with very high noise levels for short periods of time and with ear defenders.

You can find general decibel exposure time guidelines in the *Code of Safe Working Practices for Merchant Seafarers* (COSWP).

Check: is there a noise problem onboard?

Any one of these can indicate a problem with noise onboard:

- ☐ You must shout to be heard clearly by someone standing 2 metres away.
- ☐ Your ears are ringing after leaving the workplace.
- ☐ There is loud machinery or equipment running in a small space.

Be vigilant!

If you or a crewmate can hear sounds that aren't from your surroundings in one or both of your/their ears, seek help from a medical professional as soon as possible. This may be tinnitus and may be a sign of hearing loss.

Tips for working with noise

✔ **Always wear the correct PPE**, eg ear plugs or protective earmuffs.

✔ **Check company risk assessments referring to noise.**

✔ **Check how much time you should be spending around equipment that causes noise.** This should be in the risk assessment or company policy.

✔ **Recognise signs of hearing loss** and seek medical help quickly.

✔ If noise is keeping you awake, wear **ear plugs or try mindfulness and breathing exercises** (see section A.2 of the appendix). **You can also try using apps that play sounds to help you sleep.**

✔ If you believe that there is a serious problem with noise onboard, **you should report it to your company immediately.** They may be able to do something about it.

1.11   Infectious diseases

Infection can spread easily through direct contact with a contaminated person/item or through the air – for example, when someone coughs or sneezes and you inhale.

As a seafarer, you may travel to many different parts of the world for work. Onboard, you're in close proximity to fellow crew members. This can put you at greater risk of catching infectious diseases.

Poor hygiene practices onboard can also put you at risk of catching an infectious disease. To learn more about personal hygiene, read section 1.4.

There are many different infectious diseases and they all have different symptoms. **Your company should tell you where you're going and what you can expect.**

You can find up-to-date information and advice on infectious diseases in different parts of the world at **https://www.gov.uk/ foreign-travel-advice**

You can also find more general advice about infectious diseases in the *Ship Captain's Medical Guide,* which may be carried onboard your ship.

Tips for avoiding infectious disease

Before you travel:

✔ **Make sure your company has told you where you're going.**

✔ **Research the places you'll be travelling to.** Visit **https://www.gov.uk/foreign-travel-advice** to find out if you need any vaccinations and write down any tips for travel in these areas.

✔ **Get the correct vaccinations or update your vaccinations.** You should do this at least one month before travel. If you're unsure what vaccinations you need, speak to your doctor.

Tips continue on next page

While you're travelling:

✔ **Wear insect repellent.** Insects like mosquitoes can spread disease.

✔ **Only eat food from clean, hygienic places.** Avoid street vendors and food that has been left out in the open. Only eat in places that are highly recommended by travel companies or locals.

✔ **Only drink bottled water and avoid ice in drinks.** Some countries don't have safe drinking water, so you should avoid tap water.

✔ **Maintain a high standard of personal hygiene.** See section 1.4 for more information.

1.12   Sexuality

Sexuality can be an important part of a person's identity. It includes gender identity and sexual orientation.

Gender identity refers to the label you might use to describe your gender: man, woman, cisgender, transgender, etc.

Sexual orientation refers to the features you might find attractive in a potential partner. For example, you may describe yourself as gay/homosexual or straight/heterosexual.

Sexuality can change or stay the same over time.

There are many ways in which people identify their sexuality. You can see some of these in Table 1.4.

Be aware that Table 1.4 is not a complete list of all the ways in which individuals identify their sexuality.

You should never assume someone's sexuality based on what you believe you know.

Table 1.4 Sexual identity

Identity	Meaning
Straight/heterosexual	An individual who is attracted to people of the opposite gender, eg a woman who is attracted to men.
Homosexual	An individual who is attracted to people of the same gender, eg a man who is attracted to other men, or a woman who is attracted to other women.
Gay	Generally means the same as homosexual.
Lesbian	A woman who is attracted to other women.
Bisexual	An individual who is attracted to people of either gender, eg a man who is bisexual may be attracted to women or men.

Table continues on next page

Table 1.4 Sexual identity, continued

Identity	Meaning
Asexual	An individual who may not be attracted to others sexually or who may have no intention to act upon their attraction to others sexually.
Queer/questioning	An individual who chooses not to label their sexuality, as they believe that their sexuality is fluid.
Transgender	An individual whose gender at birth is different from what they believe their gender to be, eg someone who is born female physically but feels that they are male.
Cisgender	An individual whose gender at birth is the same as they believe their gender to be.
Intersex	An individual who is born with the features of both male and female genders.

1.12.1 Sexuality and the law

LGBTQIA+ stands for those who identify as lesbian, gay, bisexual, transgender, queer, intersex, asexual and other.

Unfortunately, not everyone is tolerant of the differences in sexuality. In some countries, LGBTQIA+ communities are persecuted. The punishment can range from fines to prison sentences and cruel treatment.

You may also encounter crew members who are hostile towards individuals who express different sexual identities or orientations. This is not acceptable behaviour. For more information, read section 2.4.

Tips for safe travel

✔ **Do some background research on the countries you'll be visiting.** Unfortunately, not all countries are tolerant of the LGBTQIA+ community. Some countries are hostile towards unmarried couples in general.

✔ **Make sure your passport reflects who you are now.** Some transgender individuals find it difficult to travel if their passport contains their pre-transition picture, gender marker and name. You should be able to change these through your home country's consulate. If this isn't possible, carry proof linking you to your previous identity, such as previous pictures and medical certificates. Your consulate should be able to advise you appropriately.

List continues on next page

Tips for safe travel, *continued*

✔ Ignore any unwelcome attention to your sexual identity or sexual orientation and move to a safer place.

✔ Some countries carry out entrapment campaigns for those who identify as homosexual. Always be aware of the politics around this.

✔ Be aware that some countries have low tolerance for public displays of affection, regardless of the sexual identity and orientation of those involved.

✔ Be aware that, in some countries, laws and attitudes towards men and women differ. Some countries expect women to behave and dress more conservatively than men. Do some research before you travel, to find out what is and isn't tolerated.

1.13   Relationships

Many seafarers leave loved ones behind and maintain long-distance relationships.

Maintaining a long-distance relationship can be difficult for you and your partner. It can be hard to make time for each other when you're physically apart and have different schedules.

Tips for maintaining long-distance relationships

- ✔ **Be open about what both of you want and need.** Make sure you and your partner set ground rules for what is and isn't acceptable within the relationship, and stick to these. This will build trust and help avoid disagreements.

- ✔ **Organise contact times in a way that works for both of you.** Being in different time zones and having different work schedules can make it difficult to plan when you contact each other. Make sure you pre-plan a contact schedule that works for both of you.

- ✔ **Socialise with others.** Don't become overly reliant on communicating with your partner. You should still make time to socialise with crewmates and friends.

- ✔ **Focus on quality communication.** Make a list of the things you want to tell your partner about. This will help you share things that are important to you.

- ✔ **Build trust.** When you communicate, make sure it's focused on sharing experiences, rather than checking up on what the other person has been doing. If you or your partner feel insecure, discuss this and try to overcome it.

- ✔ **Take something that reminds you of your partner.** It might not always be possible to communicate, but having something like a picture of your partner might help when you miss them.

1.13.1   Romantic relationships with other crew members

Depending on the company that you work for, your right to instigate a romantic relationship with a crewmate may be determined by the employee code of conduct.

Working with someone who you're romantically involved with can sometimes cause difficulties on a ship. This can be awkward – not just for you but for your crewmates too.

Tips for maintaining a relationship onboard

✔ **Familiarise yourself with the employee code of conduct.** Make sure that you take the necessary steps to abide by it.

✔ **Don't let your relationship affect your work.** At work, you should maintain your professionalism and act as crewmates, not partners. No-one should be able to guess your relationship status without being told. This is particularly important if you or your partner are in a management position. You shouldn't be given special treatment at work if your partner is in a position of power, or vice versa.

✔ **Don't discuss your relationship while you're at work.**

✔ **Resolve disagreements quickly.**

✔ **Treat other crew members with respect.** You shouldn't let your beliefs about other crew members affect how you or your partner treat them, and vice versa.

✔ **Communicate.** Make sure you and your partner set ground rules for what is and isn't acceptable at work and within the relationship. This will help avoid disagreements.

1.14   Sex

Sexual health means the mental, physical and social wellbeing associated with your sexuality.

To understand sexuality, read section 1.12.

Sex affects more than just your physical health. If you're engaging in sexual activity, it's important that you're open and honest with your partner about your needs, wishes and feelings.

Taking responsibility for your sexual health is the first and most important step in enjoying your sex life.

1.14.1   Consent

Before engaging in any sexual activity, you should make sure that you've gained consent from the other person involved.

Consent is about making sure that you and the person you want to engage with are completely comfortable and in agreement about your behaviour towards each other.

Consent should be gained every time, for every sexual act.

You should not assume consent:

- based on how someone is dressed
- based on past behaviour (eg they've kissed you or had sex with you in the past)
- if they've consented after drinking alcohol or taking drugs
- if they've said yes because they felt pressured
- if they haven't said 'no' or 'stop'.

You should be mindful of body language and realise when someone doesn't want to continue. If the other person pushes or pulls away, goes completely still or shivers/shakes, you should stop.

Consent still applies to sex with your long-term partner (eg husband/wife, boyfriend/girlfriend).

The age of consent is the minimum age that someone must be before they can legally agree to sexual activity.

If you or the other person are below the age of consent, you or they might be committing statutory rape. Statutory rape is a very serious and punishable crime.

The age of consent varies between countries. If you're in international waters (high seas), the age of consent in your flag state applies.

Check: have I gained consent?

When you're engaging in positive, consensual sexual activity, you should be able to tick all of these off the list:

- ☐ The individual is above the minimum age of consent.
- ☐ They're enthusiastic/happy to be with you.
- ☐ They've indicated verbally and non-verbally that they want the same things as you.
- ☐ They aren't drinking alcohol or taking drugs.
- ☐ They're active and engaged in the activity with you.
- ☐ They're comfortable telling you to stop.
- ☐ You haven't pressured or 'guilted' them into this.

Tips for giving and ensuring that you have consent

✔ **Make sure you ask questions**, such as 'Is this okay?', 'Are you comfortable with this?' or 'Do you want to stop?'

✔ **Make sure the other person can clearly communicate their needs to you**, ie they're sober, able to give consent and don't feel pressured, scared, embarrassed, etc.

✔ Make sure you can **clearly communicate your needs** to your partner, ie you're sober and don't feel pressured, scared, embarrassed, etc.

✔ Avoid anyone who ignores your verbal or non-verbal messages to stop, gets angry or reacts negatively to your saying no, or 'guilts' you into saying yes.

✔ If someone asks you to stop, then stop.

✔ **Be aware of body language**. Sometimes people are too scared or overwhelmed to say anything verbally to make you stop.

Giving consent

You have the right to choose what you would and wouldn't like to do when engaging in sexual activity.

You can withdraw consent at any time. You don't have to go through with something if you change your mind.

You shouldn't feel forced or talked into giving consent. It should be given freely and enthusiastically.

Unfortunately, you may be put in a position where someone doesn't stop when you tell them to. This isn't your fault. Try to get away. If you weren't able to get away, you may want to read section 2.5.

Remember: you may not have the power to stop someone else, but you always have the power to stop yourself.

1.14.2 Avoiding unwanted pregnancy

If you want to avoid getting pregnant yourself, or you want to avoid getting someone else pregnant, make sure you use contraception (see Table 1.5). You should seek medical advice for the best option for you.

Contraception is the responsibility of everyone who chooses to have sex. You can't rely on the other person to take precautions for you.

Remember: not all contraceptive methods protect against sexually transmitted diseases.

Although contraceptives are generally effective when used correctly, they aren't 100% reliable. This means there is a small chance that pregnancy can occur even when you use contraceptives.

If you're female, have unprotected sex, and wish to avoid pregnancy, there are various methods to prevent or terminate pregnancy. These shouldn't be used as a long-term solution.

Table 1.6 lists some of the methods that can be used to prevent pregnancy after unprotected sex

Table 1.5 Methods of contraception

Male ♂		
Method	Description	Use
Condom	A thin sheath worn over the penis during sex. Helps protect against sexually transmitted diseases (STDs) and pregnancy if used correctly.	You'll need a new condom each time you have sex. You should dispose of used condoms immediately after intercourse.
Female ♀		
Method	Description	Use
Contraceptive pill	There are many different types of contraceptive pill. When taken correctly, these release hormones that prevent pregnancy.	Most types of contraceptive pill need to be taken every day, at the same time of day, to work effectively. You should discuss your contraceptive pill with a doctor and read the instructions carefully.

Table continues on next page

Table 1.5 Methods of contraception, continued

Female ♀		
Method	**Description**	**Use**
Contraceptive injection	An injection of hormones that prevent pregnancy.	The effects can last 8–13 weeks.
Contraceptive implant	A small plastic rod that is placed under the skin. It releases hormones that prevent pregnancy.	The effects usually last for 3 years.
Intra-uterine device (IUD)	A small device that is inserted into the woman's uterus to prevent pregnancy.	The effects can last 5–10 years.
Femidom (female condom)	A small condom that is inserted into the vagina to prevent pregnancy. Helps protect against sexually transmitted diseases (STDs) and pregnancy if used correctly.	You'll need a new femidom each time you have sex. You should dispose of used femidoms immediately after intercourse.

Table 1.6 Avoiding pregnancy after unprotected sex

Method	Description	When method can be used
Emergency contraception tablet (morning after pill)	Tablet to be taken after unprotected sex. Prevents pregnancy from occurring.	Can be used up to 5 days after unprotected sex.
Emergency IUD	IUD that is fitted into the uterus. Prevents pregnancy from occurring.	Can be fitted up to 5 days after unprotected sex.
Abortion pill	1 or 2 tablets taken after pregnancy has occurred.	Can be used up to the 24th week of pregnancy.
Surgical abortion	Minor surgery that removes the pregnancy.	Can be used up to the 24th week of pregnancy.

Being at sea can make it difficult to obtain contraceptives or terminations when needed. It's important to make sure that you have long-term pregnancy prevention methods in place before you go onboard.

You can find out if you're pregnant by arranging a test through a doctor onshore.

If you can't get to a doctor, you can purchase a pregnancy test in most onshore pharmacies. It's best to follow up the test with your doctor, as these tests aren't always 100% accurate.

Be careful: abortion is a criminal offence in some countries. You should find out whether this is the case before looking for help onshore.

If you wish to have an abortion, you should only do this through specialist medical facilities (hospitals or clinics) in countries where abortion is legal.

Getting an abortion by other means can put your health at serious risk.

1.14.3 Sexually transmitted diseases

Regardless of your sexuality, it's important that you practise safe sex.

Unsafe sex can lead to you getting a sexually transmitted disease (STD). STDs are passed through unprotected sexual contact with an infected person.

There are many STDs. Common ones include herpes, chlamydia, HIV/AIDS and gonorrhoea. If they're spotted early, you can get effective medical treatment.

If they're left unchecked, however, they can cause infertility, impotence, cancer and sometimes death. You might also accidentally spread the STD to other people.

Common symptoms of STDs include changes in the colour and consistency of discharge from the genitals, warts around the genitals, pain or a burning sensation when urinating, and pain, swelling or itching of the genitals. You may also have no symptoms at all.

It isn't always possible to spot or find out if a potential partner might have an STD, so you should always practise safe sex.

Check: am I at risk of getting/already having an STD?

Any one of the following will put you at greater risk of already having or getting an STD. You should make sure that you have a regular STD check.

☐ You've used drugs or alcohol before engaging in sexual activity.

☐ You have multiple sexual partners.

☐ You haven't used or don't use condoms during sex.

☐ You haven't used or don't use protection during oral sex.

☐ You've had an STD in the past.

☐ You engage in sexual activity with people you've just met.

☐ You inject drugs.

☐ You have some of the symptoms mentioned above.

Tips for maintaining good sexual health

✔ Be aware that some countries ban certain methods of contraception or termination.

✔ Men can **use condoms** to protect from STDs.

✔ Women can **use femidoms** to protect from STDs.

✔ **Dental dams** can be used during oral sex to protect from STDs.

✔ **Check your sexual health status regularly** (before contact with any new partner). You can get an STD check through health professionals such as doctors and nurses.

✔ **You should only engage in unprotected sexual contact if you're sure of your own and your partner's sexual health status.**

1.15   Pregnancy

1.15.1   Managing pregnancy onboard

Pregnancy can be an exciting time for many. As a seafarer, you'll need to consider things that others might take for granted.

Your maternity- and paternity-related employment rights will depend on the flag state of your vessel.

You should be able to get more information from the official government website of your flag state or from your employer's pregnancy/maternity/parenthood policy.

If you find out that you're pregnant, you should tell your employer. Your company should have a policy that states when you should let them know about your pregnancy.

Letting your employer know is important. It helps them put in place procedures to protect you and your baby.

If you don't want anyone else to know about your pregnancy, your employer should respect your wishes. However, you should be aware that colleagues may guess if your workload is changed.

Some of your duties may be considered unsafe to carry out while pregnant, so your workload might have to change.

You may be able to work onshore with the organisation until the start of your maternity leave. You should speak with your employers to explore this option.

Speak with your doctor early on to identify and evaluate any risks to yourself and the baby that are associated with your job.

You shouldn't be discriminated against or dismissed from your job because of your pregnancy.

You're protected from discrimination on the grounds of your pregnancy by the ILO Maternity Protection Convention, 2000 (No. 183): **http://www.ilo.ch/global/standards/subjects-covered-by-international-labour-standards/maternity-protection/lang--en/index.htm.**

Tips for managing pregnancy

✔ Find out your maternity rights according to the flag state of the vessel.

✔ Let your organisation know as soon as possible.

✔ If you have concerns about carrying out any of your normal duties while pregnant, speak to a doctor as soon as possible. You may be able to obtain a medical certificate to exempt you from some duties.

✔ If you're working at sea for long periods of time without access to a doctor, speak to your organisation about allowing you enough time to attend check-ups during shore leave.

✔ Make sure that you attend any check-ups and screenings before you go to sea. This will let you know if you need to take extra care.

✔ Follow general advice on keeping yourself and the baby healthy. This might mean making changes to your lifestyle. Try to eat healthily (see section 1.1 for tips on a healthy diet), stop smoking and avoid alcohol and drugs (see section 3.4 for advice on quitting and addiction). Also check whether it's safe to take any medication (painkillers, vitamins, etc.).

✔ As your pregnancy progresses, you may need to purchase maternity clothes to stay comfortable while you work.

✔ Take extra care with your personal hygiene. Pregnancy can make you more vulnerable to infections. See section 1.4 for tips on maintaining your personal hygiene.

✔ Read books and download apps that give you information about your pregnancy. This can be a great way to stay informed when you're at sea and away from medical professionals, family and friends.

1.15.2 When your partner is pregnant

If you're separated from your pregnant partner, you might feel anxious for them or feel as if you're missing out. These feelings are normal.

> **Tips for managing separation from your pregnant partner**
> ✔ **Find out your paternity/maternity rights according to the flag state of your vessel.**
> ✔ **Stay in touch.** Prearrange times with your partner, so they'll be available when you contact them.
> ✔ **Make sure you and your partner have a support network.** Being separated during this time can be difficult but you'll both feel better if you know there are people around each of you who can support and take care of you.
> ✔ **Plan!** Make sure that you and your partner have an emergency plan detailing the people your partner can contact in an emergency or when they're due to give birth. The people involved in this plan should be told, so that they're prepared to be contacted.
> ✔ **If something is worrying you, talk about it.** This can be an anxious time for you and your partner. If something happens to worry you, talk to someone onboard who you trust. Sharing your burden can sometimes be enough to help you get through a difficult time.
> ✔ **Get informed about pregnancy and parenthood.** You might feel more involved and in control if you know what's happening during and after pregnancy. You can support your partner by understanding their needs and asking the right questions even if you're not physically there.

2 Personal and social wellbeing

2.1 Communication

Living and working closely with other crew members can be tricky if you don't communicate well.

Good communication is important for your work and social life.

By learning to communicate properly, you can reduce misunderstandings and settle conflicts quickly before they get out of control.

Tips for effective communication

✔ **Remember body language.** What you do with your body can tell someone a lot about what you're trying to say, so make sure you keep your body relaxed and open when you're talking, as shown in Figure 2.1:

  – Leaning in slightly can show that you're interested in the conversation, while leaning away can show that you aren't listening.

  – Crossing your arms can act as a barrier, like you're shutting yourself off from the conversation. Try having your arms comfortably at your sides.

  – Make sure you don't gesture too much. It can be distracting.

  – Keep a comfortable level of eye contact. Don't stare at the other person.

  – Don't fidget, yawn or fake a smile.

Tips continue on next page

✔ **Don't interrupt when someone else is talking** – unless it's an emergency and what you have to say is important.

✔ **Listen**. Don't just think about what you want to say. Really listen to the other person. Ask them questions about things they've said to show them that you're interested.

✔ **Don't be aggressive**. Make sure you're not attacking someone with your words or body language. People are more likely to listen to you if you're calm.

2.1.1   Verbal and non-verbal communication

Communication isn't just about what you say. It's also about how you say it. Communication can be verbal (with words) or non-verbal (with your body).

The way you communicate can depend on many things, like your abilities and culture, so be mindful of this. Read section 2.2 to see how culture might affect communication.

These tips are just for guidance. **It's important that you actively listen during a conversation, so don't focus too much on displaying the right body language.**

Just try to improve the things you might be doing wrong.

Be aware that emotions can spread. If you're in a bad mood and communicate this, physically and verbally, it can put others in a bad mood too!

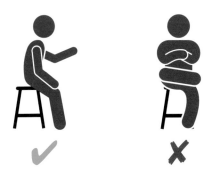

Figure 2.1 Open (left) versus defensive (right) body language

2.1.2   Teamwork

Communication is vital for teamwork.

Being part of a crew means that you're always working as part of a team.

A team is a group of people who work together to achieve a common goal.

You don't necessarily have to have a good personal relationship with someone to work well with them, but it does help.

Try to build relationships with the people you see every day. This will make teamwork easier. You can get to know people by following the tips in this section and in section 2.3.

Tips for working in a team

✔ **Make sure you have the same goals at work**. If you don't already have them, suggest regular meetings and handovers to make sure you're all working towards the same thing.

✔ **Get to know people**. Take time to introduce yourself to other crew members and ask them questions about themselves.

✔ **Respect everyone**. Everyone has ideas and experience that they can bring to a team. You should treat everyone equally and give everyone respect.

✔ **Build trust**. Be reliable. If you say that you're going to do something, then do it.

✔ **Be helpful**. Try to help other crew members when you can.

2.1.3   Conflict

Sometimes, communication can get out of hand and lead to conflict. Conflict can get out of control quickly.

Common causes of conflict onboard include miscommunication, work pressures or simply having little privacy.

It's easy to become annoyed at someone if you can't get away from them and have space to clear your mind. Read section 2.3 to find out how you can get some privacy onboard.

Be vigilant!

It's not always possible to stop a conflict from escalating once it has begun. It's better to try to prevent the conflict from occurring in the first place.

Try to be aware of your crewmates' moods and feelings on a day-to-day basis. If you know that someone has had a bad day, it might not be the best time to talk to them about something that might make them feel worse.

Pay attention to your own moods and feelings too. Have you had a bad day? Does that mean you're more likely to overreact to something?

If you feel a conflict is about to happen, try to distance yourself from the situation, so that you and the other person(s) involved can have some time to think and calm down.

Tips for avoiding conflict

✔ **Keep as calm as possible.**

✔ Use the communication tips in this section.

✔ **Find out why the other person might be upset.** Use open questions to find out what's bothering them.

  – Questions that begin with 'who', 'when' or 'what' can help you gather information.

✔ **Summarise.** Once you've heard everything the other person has to say, summarise and ask them whether what you've gathered is correct.

Tips continue on next page

✔ **Acknowledge how the other person feels**. You can say things like 'I understand why you feel like this'. Apologising can also help.

✔ **Speak to your manager**. If there was a serious disagreement, let them know that a situation has occurred and seek their advice.

2.2   Cultural differences

Working at sea may bring you into contact with people from lots of different cultural backgrounds.

Culture guides your beliefs, ideas and values. Cultural diversity is important because it means that there are a range of talents, skills and experiences onboard.

We can all be sensitive about our beliefs and values. This can lead to misunderstandings, so it's important to be considerate about other people's beliefs and views.

2.2.1   Gestures

Gestures and actions can mean different things in different cultures, so be careful when using them.

Table 2.1 shows some common gestures and what they mean in different countries or cultures. This isn't a full list, so be careful when using any gesture.

Table 2.1 Common gestures and their meanings in different countries

Gesture		Meaning
Eye contact		• Asia: a sign of respect • Latin and North America: a sign of equality
Okay sign		• North America and UK: means something is okay • Japan: refers to money • Argentina, Belgium, France and Portugal: means zero • Brazil, Germany and Russia: gesture is offensive
Winking		• Latin America: is seen as a sexual invitation • China: winking is offensive/rude
Putting your leg on the opposite knee		• Middle East: considered dirty

Table continues on next page

Table 2.1 Common gestures and their meanings in different countries, continued

Gesture		Meaning
Accepting or giving things with your left hand		• Middle East and India: considered rude or unclean
Thumbs up		• UK and USA: means 'good' or 'well done' • Greece and Middle East: offensive gesture • Japan: means number 5
Pointing with index finger		• Offensive in many cultures (Asia, Europe and Latin America)
Curling the index finger with palm facing up		• USA and UK: means 'come here' or 'come closer' • Asia: offensive or rude gesture
Upright, open hand with fingers apart		• Western cultures: hello or greeting • Greece, Pakistan, Persian Gulf and Mexico: rude gesture

If you're offended by a gesture that your colleague has made, don't jump to conclusions. Take the time to explain what it means in your culture. They probably didn't realise it was offensive.

Tips for communicating with people from different cultures

✔ Be careful how you use words or actions in a conversation.

✔ **Get to know your crewmates**. Once you have a good relationship, it will be easier to avoid misunderstandings.

✔ Learn what is and isn't acceptable in different cultures.

✔ **Speak clearly**. Don't shout or talk down to the other person.

✔ **Don't judge.** You shouldn't assume something about someone just because of their culture, how they look, their age, etc. Try to get to know them before you make any judgements. Something that may seem odd to you might be normal in their culture.

✔ Learn how to pronounce your crewmates' names correctly.

✔ Be aware of and respect cultural or religious holidays and prayer times.

✔ Be interested in others' experiences.

2.3   Loneliness

Humans are generally social animals, meaning that we need to interact with others to be happy.

Loneliness is when you feel down because you feel that you have no company.

Loneliness and isolation are different. Isolation is to do with how many people you have contact with. The more isolated you are, the fewer people you see or talk to.

You might be isolated and not feel lonely because you have very good relationships with the people you do see. However, you can see or talk to people often and still feel lonely because you haven't got many quality relationships.

Loneliness can affect both your mental and physical health, making it difficult to carry out day-to-day tasks by reducing your motivation.

Signs of loneliness include:

*   Homesickness
*   Low motivation
*   Social withdrawal/isolation
*   Sadness/low mood
*   Loss of appetite.

Tips to overcome loneliness

✔ **Take the initiative** and introduce yourself to other people. Learn their names and use them in conversation.

✔ **Eat meals with your crewmates** in the communal area.

✔ **Plan for the journey**. Download books, playlists, movies and games to enjoy with your crewmates.

✔ **Use social media** to keep updated on your family and friends, but don't rely on it. Make sure you still form relationships with other crew members.

✔ **Exercise!** It can give you a focus and direction and can help you meet new people.

Tips for helping a lonely crew member

✔ **Tell them you're there for them**. Let the person know you're around if they need you, and try to engage them in social situations where possible, eg exercise, a walk around the ship or eating together in the mess.

✔ **Encourage them to make new connections**. Sometimes people just need confidence to make new friends and take up new activities. Try introducing them to crew members with similar interests or involving them in social situations.

✔ **Be patient**. It may take some time for the person to gain confidence or engage with others. You may feel frustrated because it doesn't seem as if they're trying. Give them time and try not to push them to do things too fast. Let them set the pace.

2.3.1   Getting privacy

Being alone can sometimes be very therapeutic.

Living in close quarters with other crew members may make you feel like you don't get much time to be on your own. Sometimes this can be overwhelming.

Spending time alone is important for your wellbeing. It can help you to relax, solve problems and even improve your concentration.

> Tips for spending time alone onboard
>
> ✔ **Let your crewmates know** when you don't want to be disturbed.
>
> ✔ **Switch off your personal devices**: mobile phone, laptop, etc.
>
> ✔ **Use headphones** to drown out any background noise during breaks.
>
> ✔ **Do something you enjoy.** Sometimes, just doing an activity (eg exercise) by yourself can give you space to think.

2.4 Bullying, harassment and discrimination

Bullying is when a person abuses their power or influence to humiliate or hurt someone in some way.

Bullies tend to have more power than their victim. They may be physically stronger or they may just be in a position of greater influence.

Discrimination is when a person treats someone else unfairly because of a personal characteristic, eg gender, race, disability or religion.

Harassment can include bullying and discrimination, but it happens when one person abuses another because of a specific characteristic (gender, race, disability, religion, etc.).

Your company has a responsibility to ensure that bullying, harassment and discrimination are dealt with appropriately if they occur.

You should be aware of what counts as bullying and harassment, so that you can spot when others do it, or when you're bullying/ harassing someone yourself, and stop it.

Check: are you being bullied/are you a bully?

Any of these behaviours counts as bullying if it happens more than once, targeting one specific person or group of people:

- ☐ Verbally or physically threatening someone
- ☐ Verbally or physically abusing people: swearing, hitting, etc.
- ☐ Making personal insults
- ☐ Putting someone down or mocking them
- ☐ Being unreasonably critical of someone or their abilities
- ☐ Making unreasonable demands
- ☐ Setting tasks that are too simple or inappropriate for someone's job
- ☐ Ignoring or excluding people
- ☐ Spreading rumours
- ☐ Discriminating against someone due to their characteristics eg race, gender, age etc.
- ☐ Doing any of the above online or using technology (cyber bullying).

Check: are you being harassed by/harassing someone?

Any of these behaviours counts as harassment if it happens more than once, targeting one specific person or group of people:

- ☐ Making inappropriate jokes or remarks, eg sexist/racist/homophobic comments
- ☐ Showing people offensive material, eg pornographic images
- ☐ Spying on, stalking or pestering people
- ☐ Making or sending unwanted sexual, intimidating or personally inappropriate messages
- ☐ Making unwelcome sexual advances or threats
- ☐ Initiating unnecessary bodily contact with someone
- ☐ Insulting someone or spreading rumours about them based on their personal characteristics (gender, sexuality, etc.)
- ☐ Suggesting that sexual favours can further someone's career.

Tips for dealing with bullying/harassment/discrimination

✔ **Read through your company's policy on bullying, harassment and discrimination.** Note down what you need to do.

✔ **Keep calm and be firm.** Try to stay confident and make your feelings about the situation clear.

✔ **Keep a record of incidents.** Note the time, date, place, what happened, and the people involved on your phone or in a diary.

✔ **Make your manager aware of the situation.** You can make a formal complaint if you want to.

✔ **Check your job description** to confirm whether you've been set tasks that are too simple or unfair.

✔ **Speak to colleagues** to see whether they saw the incident or have been affected too. It can help to get other people's perspective on the situation.

✔ If you complain, keep **your explanation factual.** Don't use aggressive or emotional language.

✔ **Alert the company** if your claims aren't taken seriously. Email them if possible, so you have a record of the complaints you've made.

Check: are you being discriminated against/discriminating?

Any of these behaviours counts as discrimination if it happens more than once, targeting one specific person or group of people:

- [ ] Treating someone/a group of people poorly or not as well as others because of a personal characteristic
- [ ] Excluding someone because of a personal characteristic
- [ ] Assuming negative things about a person because of a personal characteristic
- [ ] Using stereotypes.

Sometimes, discrimination, bullying and harassment can escalate and lead to violence. Read section 2.5.4 for advice on assault and rape.

2.5   Crime

Being the victim of a crime is often a traumatic experience. You might not have much time to think or react while the crime is happening, so it's important to know what you should do afterwards.

If you're the victim of a crime, it isn't your fault.

You can take some steps to increase your personal security, but ultimately the person responsible for the crime is the one who commits it.

Remember:

- **In port or onshore, the laws that apply will be those of the country you're in.**

- In open water, the laws that apply will be those of your vessel's flag state.

2.5.1   Theft

If you take something that belongs to someone else without permission and for your own gain, this counts as theft.

Living in close quarters with little privacy, travelling to different countries and having frequent changes of crew can mean that you're constantly around new people in unfamiliar places.

If the theft happens onshore, you should report it to the local police.

If the theft happens onboard, you should report it to management.

Punishment for stealing can include imprisonment, amputation or even death, depending on the country in which the crime occurs.

> Tips for avoiding theft
> Onboard:
> ✔ **Lock up important belongings.** There should be a place in your cabin where you can securely store your belongings.
> ✔ **Don't tell other crew members where you keep important belongings.** Even if you're telling people you trust, you might be overheard.
> ✔ **Don't bring anything onboard that can't be replaced.** Try to leave valuables at home. Consider buying a cheap mobile phone, MP3 player, etc. that you can replace easily if it's lost or stolen.
> ✔ **Take copies of important documents (eg passport) and leave a copy behind with relatives.**

Onshore:

✔ **Try not to carry valuables in a bag.** This is an easy target for pickpockets.

✔ **Don't wear expensive jewellery/watches.**

✔ Make a note of local police telephone numbers and the number of your shipping company in case you need them.

Be vigilant!

You should always take care of important possessions, but be extra careful if:

• You or another crew member notice that supplies, equipment or possessions are going missing

• You spot people in areas they shouldn't be, at odd times.

2.5.2   Piracy

Piracy is when an individual or group attack and/or steal from a vessel at sea.

Piracy is more common in some areas than others. Over 100 piracy incidents occur each year.

As a seafarer, you're on the frontline of pirate attacks.

You and your shipping company have a responsibility to ensure you're protected from piracy as far as possible.

General advice on piracy can be found on the IMO website.

Tips for preventing piracy

✔ **Familiarise yourself with piracy hotspots.** You can find these by searching for the 'IMB Piracy Reporting Centre' online.

✔ **Read the vessel's policy on piracy,** so you know what to do in the event of an attack.

✔ **Avoid talking about your vessel to people you don't know.**

✔ **Be vigilant.** Watch out for any suspicious people or vessels.

✔ **Report any suspicious vessels to the master.**

Be vigilant!

Be suspicious of strangers who seem to be taking a lot of interest in you, asking you lots of questions or following you.

If you suspect that someone intends to harm you, then try to distance yourself.

Criminals are often very good at hiding in plain sight, so just be careful not to say or do anything that could put you or your vessel in danger.

Suspicious vessels may have any of the following features:

• The vessel is unmarked, or its name is on a removable device or equipment

• It moves in unusual ways or it does not seem to have a set course

• It doesn't have or use any running/navigational lights

• There may be smaller vessels grouped around a larger one.

After an attack

Experiencing a pirate attack can be traumatic.

Make sure you get medical care if you need it. Your company should organise medical care, but if it doesn't, you can get help from some of the contacts listed in section A.5 of the appendix.

If you feel that you've been mentally and emotionally affected, read section 3.7.2 on post-traumatic stress disorder. You can also use the contacts in section A.5 of the appendix to talk to someone about the incident.

Your company procedure should detail how the incident should be reported and dealt with.

A full investigation of the attack will be conducted at the next or nearest port. You should be ready to answer questions if necessary. Make sure you stick to the facts when answering questions.

2.5.3   Assault

Assault refers to physical attack.

If you're attacked onboard, report it to management immediately.

If you're attacked onshore, report it to the local authorities immediately.

Assault can happen for various reasons, either on its own or in combination with another crime (eg theft). You can't always stop an assault from occurring, but there are some steps you can take to increase your personal safety.

Tips for personal safety onshore

✔ **Avoid alcohol and drugs.** Even a small quantity of alcohol or drugs can affect your decision-making skills.

✔ **Be aware of your surroundings.**

✔ **Stay in well-lit and busy areas.** However, make sure you keep alert for pickpockets, as they tend to operate in busy areas.

✔ **Carry a personal alarm.**

✔ **Don't let strangers buy you drinks.** They could be laced with drugs, eg the date-rape drug.

✔ **Avoid going anywhere alone.** Travel as a group and look out for each other when possible.

2.5.4   Sexual assault and rape

Rape occurs when sex is non-consensual. (Read section 1.14.1 to understand consent.)

Sexual assault refers to non-consensual sexual acts other than sex, eg inappropriate touching or kissing.

Anyone can be a victim of rape or sexual assault. It doesn't depend on gender, sexuality, age or anything else.

Rape and sexual assault are violent crimes; the rapist is responsible for the attack because the rapist always has a choice. The victim doesn't have a choice.

If you've been raped or sexually assaulted, it's up to you how and if you decide to tell anyone. Do what you feel is right for you: by taking control, you're taking the first step towards recovery.

Everyone reacts differently during and after rape or sexual assault. Your priority should be your own wellbeing.

It may not be easy for you to avoid the rapist/offender if they're onboard. If this is the case, consider reporting the person to the company or management to put some distance between you.

Your company should take rape and sexual assault allegations seriously.

What to do if you've been raped or sexually assaulted

- **Go to a safe place.** This may not always be possible onboard a vessel, but try to get yourself away from the perpetrator. If the incident didn't occur in your room, then you may choose to go there.

- **Don't blame yourself.** This isn't your fault. You didn't have a choice in this.

- **Seek medical help.** Even if you choose not to talk about the incident, you may want to make sure that your injuries are treated. This isn't just about the physical effects but also the mental effects of the incident. For further advice suiting your needs, you can refer to the list of contacts in section A.5 of the appendix.

- **Think about telling someone.** You may feel better if there is someone to reassure and help you through this. They may not necessarily be onboard with you.

What to do if a colleague/friend tells you they've been assaulted or raped

- **Listen.** Don't interrupt but show that you're listening.
- **Let them decide what to do.** Don't get angry or try to force them to do something they don't want to do. Let them take control of the situation. Support them in their decisions.
- **Take it seriously.** Your colleague/friend needs support. Reassure them that you believe them. It takes bravery to talk about rape or sexual assault, and they're putting their trust in you.
- **Don't blame them for the incident.** The perpetrator would have raped/assaulted regardless of how your colleague/friend behaved or dressed.

Collecting evidence

If you decide to report the incident to senior management and/or law enforcement, there are some things you can do to prove that the incident happened.

Rape is illegal in most countries, so you shouldn't be put off reporting the incident if you want to.

Advice for collecting evidence

1) **Seek advice from law enforcement authorities**. You should try to make contact with flag-state or port-state law enforcement authorities for advice on how to collect evidence and to make an initial report of the crime.

2) **Avoid washing after the incident**. You may feel unclean and want to wash, but swabs taken from the genitals or anus can provide evidence that can be matched to the rapist. Evidence may also be collected from under your fingernails.

   – Swabs should be taken by a medical professional with forensic training. This should be arranged after you've reported the crime. They will know what to do with the evidence.

   – If you don't have access to a medical professional, you can take internal swabs yourself. These should be packaged separately and frozen.

3) **Save any clothing from the incident**. Store it in a paper bag. If the clothes are damp or wet let them air dry first. Do not put the clothes in the washing machine or in a dryer. This may destroy evidence.

4) **Take photos of any injuries, immediately after the attack and at any point when new injuries appear**. Keep these in a safe place and give them to the authorities as soon as possible.

Advice continues on next page

5) **Get access to emergency contraception and STD checks if necessary** (see section 1.14).

6) **Make a note of any witnesses.** Note down anyone who may be able to support your evidence.

7) **If this is a repeated incident, record times, dates, locations and anyone who may have seen the attack.**

2.5.5   Criminalisation

When a serious maritime incident occurs, you may find yourself in a situation where you must defend yourself against criminal charges.

The IMO/ILO Guidelines on the Fair Treatment of Seafarers in the Event of a Maritime Accident set out internationally agreed standards to ensure you're treated fairly during an investigation.

However, these guidelines aren't always enforced. So, it's important that you're aware of your rights when an incident occurs. Your country's embassies or consulates can help with this.

Advice for dealing with a maritime investigation

- **Ask for a lawyer before answering questions or making statements to any investigating authority.** You should do this even if you don't feel that you need a lawyer. What you say could be used as evidence against you, so it's important that you take steps to protect yourself as far as possible.

- **Contact your union for legal advice as soon as possible.** It's helpful to have the support of a union if your company isn't able to help. You can also find some legal advice at **https://www.itfseafarers.org**

- **If you don't understand what is happening or what you're being asked, ask for the questioning to be stopped.** Make sure you state that you don't understand the questions. You can ask for an interpreter if you need one.

2.6 Whistle-blowing

Whistle-blowing is when you reveal information about an illegal, unethical or incorrect action or actions carried out in your organisation.

Most of the time, whistle-blowing is anonymous. This means that you don't have to share your identity if you don't want to.

Your company should have a whistle-blowing or grievance policy that states what you should report, who you should report it to, and how (by phone, internet, etc.).

If your company doesn't have a whistle-blowing policy, you may be able to report the action(s) to a relevant authority, such as the flag-state government, the National Whistleblower Center or the IMO.

You can get more advice about whistle-blowing from
https://www.whistleblowers.org/know-your-rights/

Check: should you blow the whistle?

☐ I have proof that the vessel/organisation is involved in unethical or illegal activity, eg pollution, drug and or/ human trafficking, abuse of workers.

☐ The information that I give affects other people.

☐ I've looked at the company/flag-state whistle-blowing policies and procedures.

If you're able to tick every box, you should consider blowing the whistle.

Be vigilant!

If you believe that your vessel/organisation is involved in illegal or unethical activity, make sure you have proof.

If you decide to blow the whistle, make sure that you follow the policy and procedure for whistle-blowing set by your organisation or flag state.

You may want to be discreet about whistle-blowing if you think that your organisation might try to punish you for reporting the illegal or unethical activity.

Be aware that you might not be able to stay anonymous throughout the process if your evidence is required to prosecute the organisation.

2.7   Finance

Managing your money can be difficult, even when you have steady work. Learning how to keep on top of your finances can help you stay well.

Your pay schedule will depend on your employer. You should make sure you're clear about when and how much you'll be paid before you begin work.

Budgeting might be particularly difficult if you send money home or have long periods of work followed by long periods without work. It's important that you consider these factors when you're looking for work. Be realistic about how much you need to live on and support your family.

You should be in control of your finances even while you're at sea. This might mean signing up for internet banking services if these are offered by your bank.

It might be tempting to trust relatives with your finances, but they may not always know the best way to spend and invest your money. If you do this, trust is important. Make sure that you don't leave your finances with people who are irresponsible with money.

How to manage your finances

1) **Write down your savings target**

This is the amount you want to save each month.

Let's assume you want to save 20% of your monthly wages. You can work this out by (a) dividing your wage by 10, then (b) multiplying it by 2.

So, if you earned $1200 a month, you should aim to save $240:

    (a) 1200/10 = 120
    (b) 120 x 2 = 240

2) **Calculate your income**
Your income is all the money you've earned, eg your salary. Bank loans don't count as income because you'll have to pay them back.

3) **Add up your fixed outgoings**
These are essential expenses, or money that you must spend to be able to live comfortably. This category includes food costs, gas and electricity bills, house payments, car payments, etc.

4) **Write down your non-essential outgoings**
These are things that you spend money on but don't need, eg video games, gadgets, cinema tickets.

5) Calculate the total saved this month

You can work out how much you've saved this month by
(a) adding all your outgoings together and (b) subtracting
this amount from your monthly wage. For example, if your
total fixed outgoings were $800 and your total non-essential
outgoings were $320:

   (a) 800 + 320 = 1120

   (b) 1200 − 1120 = 80 saved

Compare the amount you've saved to your target amount.
If you haven't saved enough, examine your non-essential
outgoings to identify where you can spend less money.

Tips for managing your finances

✔ **Keep track of how much you earn and how much you
spend**. See the previous page for an easy template you can
use. There are also apps that can help you with this, but
beware of hidden or extra charges in 'free' apps.

✔ **Set a monthly budget to live on**. Be sensible with your
money; don't use it impulsively.

✔ **You can use the 50–20–30 rule**. After tax, 50% of your
income should go on things you need, 20% should be saved
and 30% can go on things you want.

✔ **Have an emergency pot of savings** in case something
goes wrong with your pay or you need money urgently.

Tips continue on next page

✔ **Make a financial plan before you go to sea**. If you have a family to support, make sure you're clear on how much money they'll need, how much you'll send them, and how you'll do this. If you trust your finances to someone else, tell them specifically what they can and can't spend money on.

2.8   Travel

Joining a vessel or travelling home can mean taking several connecting flights, which makes preparation vital.

If you're new to travelling, it's important that you prepare as much as possible before your trip. Try to do some research or ask colleagues what you can expect.

When you arrive in a new country, the chances are that you'll have a good time, but sometimes things can go wrong. Take care to keep yourself safe.

Doing some research on the countries you'll be travelling to is always a good idea.

You can usually find information on government websites or through sources such as Lonely Planet and TripAdvisor.

Tips for safe travel

Before travel:

✔ **Don't let anyone else pack your bags and don't take luggage for anyone else.** Make sure you know what is in your bags.

✔ **Check your documentation:**
   – Make sure that you have your Continuous Discharge Certificate or discharge book and passport. Make sure that your passport hasn't expired and your discharge certificate is filled out correctly.

✔ **Keep your documents in a safe place and make sure you have photocopies.** Also send photocopies to a family member and a widely accessible personal email account (eg Gmail) if possible.

✔ **Take a written list of contacts.** This should include the telephone numbers of your embassy, shipping agents and any other useful contacts.

✔ **Make sure that you take some cash with you.** Find out whether you'll need any foreign currency.

✔ **Check the laws of the country you're travelling to, and respect them.** In some countries, homosexuality, some medications, buying and using alcohol or drugs, taking pictures of law officials and other practices are banned.

Tips continue on next page

✔ **If you're on regular medication, make sure you take your prescription or a doctor's note** to show why you need it. Also, make sure you have enough medication to last the length of your contract. It's a good idea to take more than you need in case your contract is extended.

During travel:

✔ If you miss a flight, **speak to the airline staff**. Find out what your new travel arrangements will be.

✔ If the shipping agent isn't at the destination, **call the shipping agents and follow their instructions**. Don't leave the airport until they arrive.

✔ If your luggage is lost or stolen, **complete a lost or stolen luggage form with your local shipping agent**.

✔ **Let your vessel agent and the police know if you lose any documents.** See section 2.5 on crime for more information.

During travel:

✔ **Keep loose change for a payphone** in case you lose your mobile phone.

✔ **Make sure your clothing is culturally appropriate** and won't draw unwanted attention.

✔ **Don't keep all your money in one place.** Avoid putting personal possessions in bags, as they can be easy targets.

✔ **Don't use unmarked taxis.**

✔ **Avoid bargains or cheap deals.** They're usually scams.

Check: have you packed everything you'll need?

Table 2.2 isn't an exhaustive list of everything you'll need onboard, but you can use it as a starting point.

You might also be able to ask your company for advice on what you'll need to pack.

Try to come up with ways to reduce some of your baggage. For example, instead of taking a charger for each electronic device, can you take a universal charger that allows you to charge many different devices?

Table 2.2 Travel checklist

Essential documents
☐　Passport
☐　Work documentation
☐　Cash
☐　Foreign currency
☐　Debit/credit/banking cards
☐　Important phone numbers

Table continues on next page

Table 2.2 Travel checklist, continued

Garments

Essentials
- ☐ Underwear
- ☐ Socks
- ☐ Long- and short-sleeve t-shirts/tops
- ☐ Trousers

Workwear
- ☐ Work shoes
- ☐ Waterproof shoes/boots

Weather-specific
Warm weather:
- ☐ Sunglasses
- ☐ Sandals (closed-toe)
- ☐ Shorts/skirts
- ☐ Light t-shirts/vests
- ☐ Hat

Cold weather:
- ☐ Thermal layers, eg thermal vests, leggings
- ☐ Hat (thermal)
- ☐ Gloves
- ☐ Scarf
- ☐ Winter coat
- ☐ Jumpers

Culturally appropriate wear:

- ☐ Long-sleeve t-shirts/tops with high necklines
- ☐ Long trousers/skirts
- ☐ Headscarf
- ☐ Flat shoes

Toiletries

- ☐ Soap
- ☐ Toothbrush
- ☐ Toothpaste
- ☐ Razors
- ☐ Deodorant
- ☐ Nail clippers
- ☐ Sun cream
- ☐ Moisturiser
- ☐ Lip balm
- ☐ Insect repellent
- ☐ Hand sanitiser
- ☐ Towel(s)
- ☐ Sanitary towels/tampons
- ☐ Shampoo

Medical

- ☐ Medication
- ☐ Painkillers
- ☐ Travel sickness tablets
- ☐ Prescription medication
- ☐ Antiseptic cream/wipes
- ☐ Plasters
- ☐ Contraceptives

Personal items

- ☐ Photos of family/friends
- ☐ Religious/spiritual items

Table continues on next page

Table 2.2 Travel checklist, continued

Electronics	
☐ Phone and charger	☐ DVDs (and player)
☐ Laptop/tablet and charger	☐ eBook and charger
	☐ Mini fan
☐ MP3 device	☐ Portable power bank
☐ Headphones	☐ Plug converter

Other	
☐ Books	☐ Water bottle/flask
☐ Journal/notebook	☐ Cabin/day bag
☐ Pens and pencils	☐ Padlocks
☐ Ear plugs	☐ Small torch
☐ Eye mask	☐ Laundry detergent

2.9   Repatriation

You might be put in a position where you and/or your crewmates are abandoned by the shipowner.

Repatriation means returning to your home country after a period of work.

If a shipowner does any of the following to you or your crewmates, it's called abandonment:

- They don't cover the cost of your repatriation.
- They leave you without support or help to get back home.
- They don't pay your wages for at least 2 months.

It's the shipowner's duty to make sure that you aren't abandoned.

According to the Maritime Labour Convention (2006), you have the right to be repatriated at no cost to yourself if:

* Your employment agreement expires while you're onboard
* Your employment agreement is terminated by the shipowner while you're onboard
* You terminate your employment agreement (for just reasons) while you're onboard
* You're unable to carry out your duties, eg due to illness or injury
* Your vessel is shipwrecked
* Your ship is bound for a warzone and you haven't agreed to go.

Tips to deal with abandonment

✔ **Make sure your employment agreement states what will happen in the event of abandonment and the shipowner's responsibility for repatriation.** This should be signed by you and your employer.

✔ **Make a note of important contacts before you travel.** This should include contact details for your embassy, the port-state control, the ship's flag-state embassy, trade unions and other organisations, such as ITF, that can give you legal advice (see section A.5 of the appendix).

✔ **Be aware of the signs and take action.** These are detailed in the 'Be vigilant!' box.

Be vigilant!

Early signs of abandonment include:

- Wages not being paid
- Shortage of food and water onboard
- There doesn't seem to be money to pay for services and supplies provided for the ship.

If you feel that your ship might be abandoned, get advice as soon as possible. Organisations such as ITF can give you legal advice (see section A.5 of the appendix for details).

2.10   Cyber security

Thanks to technology and the internet, it's easier than ever to keep in touch with friends and family around the world.

If your vessel has a satellite internet connection, you'll be able to access the internet most of the time, in most places. Other methods of internet connection, such as dial-up or wireless devices, will work less well in open waters.

If internet connection is important to you, you should check what is available onboard and plan accordingly.

The internet is useful, but you need to be careful because connecting to people around the world can expose you to various dangers.

It doesn't matter who you are: anyone can be the target of a cyber-attack.

You should make sure that you always have anti-virus software and a firewall installed on your computer. All personal accounts should be password protected.

Tips for keeping yourself and others safe online

✔ Make sure you follow company rules for internet use and use of personal devices onboard.

✔ Update your computer's anti-virus and firewall software regularly.

✔ Don't click on links from people or companies you don't know.

✔ Don't send money to people you don't know or have never met in person. This is almost always a scam.

✔ When you do online shopping and banking, check that the website has a small padlock icon in the address bar. This means the website is safe and secure.

✔ Change your passwords regularly and make sure they don't include the names or dates of birth of loved ones or an easy sequence like 12345.

✔ If you use online banking, make sure you use the free security software that the bank offers or use a secure mobile app.

Be vigilant!

If you receive an email asking for any amount of money, or asking you to click a link, this could be a scam. Scam emails are also called 'phishing' emails.

A phishing email may:

- Include a link that differs from the one that appears when you hover the cursor over it
- Have bad grammar and spelling mistakes
- Ask for personal information
- Offer you a deal that's too good to be true.

You should also be aware of fake news: false or misleading information that could lead you to a scam.

Here are two ways to spot fake news:

- If you don't recognise the source of the news, or you don't see the story reported on a major news site, then it's probably fake.
- If the story makes far-fetched claims (eg a cure for a terminal illness or a way to get a lot of money quickly), then it's probably fake.

2.10.1   Social media

Social media can help you feel connected to your friends and family while you're at sea.

However, you need to be careful who you talk to online and who has access to your personal information.

Many normal aspects of social media can have an impact on your wellbeing. Simply having a social networking profile can expose you to:

- Trolling/cyber bullying: where people harass you online. You might not even know them personally
- Fraud/scams: when you're targeted by people who want to make money from the information they gain about you online, either by making you send money to them or by pretending to be you to gain access to your accounts, set up credit cards, etc.
- Malware: this includes viruses designed to damage your phone/laptop/PC and software designed to steal information about you
- Catfishing: when an individual pretends to be someone else to lure you into a friendship or relationship
- Content that makes you feel bad about yourself or encourages you to do something dangerous
- Fake news: deliberately shared false or inaccurate information, often connected with something in the news.

Remember: if your social media profile isn't private, anyone can see your information, including colleagues and your employer. It's important to think about this when you post anything or show support for something. Your behaviour online reflects your character and you will be judged by it.

Be careful what you post about your workplace, as people may be able to use this information to attack or harm your organisation or vessel.

Tips for using social networking sites safely

✔ **Read and put into action the tips in this section for keeping yourself and others safe online.**

✔ **Read and understand your company's policy on using social media onboard.** Make sure you don't share any information about the vessel that could undermine its security, including:

   – Location

   – Cargo

   – Security arrangements.

✔ **Keep your profile private.** This makes it more difficult for criminals to access your information.

✔ **Don't add people you don't know.** Don't let anyone you haven't met see your information. They may not be who they claim to be online.

✔ **Ask for permission before you share pictures of other crew members or the vessel.**

✔ **Avoid posting or showing support for anything that others may find distasteful, offensive or inappropriate,** even if it's a joke. This might also mean deleting things that you've posted in the past.

✔ **Don't spend too much time on social media.** Social media can be addictive. Make sure that you don't become reliant on it. Take opportunities to form real friendships onboard.

3   Mental and emotional wellbeing

3.1   Personal resilience

Personal resilience can be thought of as your ability to adapt to or bounce back from a situation that caused you emotional or mental pain.

Resilience can help you cope with situations in your day-to-day life (difficult colleagues, boredom, motivation, loneliness, etc.). It's not about ignoring or denying your emotions. It's about your ability to feel those emotions and cope with them.

Personal resilience is important for keeping yourself mentally and emotionally well, but it takes time to develop.

Some of the factors that make a person resilient include:

* A positive attitude
* The ability to cope with emotions
* The ability to see failure as a chance to learn.

Check: are you resilient?

If one or more of the following sentences apply to you, you may need to work on your resilience. You can use the tips in the box below to build your resilience.

☐   When things don't go according to plan, it affects my confidence.

☐   When things get hard, I give up quickly.

List continues on next page

Are you resilient? *(Continued)*

☐ I don't have anyone I can speak to about the things that are troubling me.

☐ I don't deal with stress well.

☐ I find it hard to ask for help.

☐ I feel overwhelmed a lot.

☐ I worry a lot.

☐ I struggle with change.

☐ I struggle with failure.

Tips for building personal resilience

✔ **Get enough sleep, eat well and exercise.**

✔ **Look at tough situations as learning curves.** Look at the things that went well and the things that didn't, and try to learn from them so you're more prepared in the future.

✔ **Try to gain some control over the situation.** What can you do to make things better for yourself? Set specific and achievable goals.

✔ **Try to stay positive.** Having a positive outlook on life can help you think about things more clearly (see section A.1 of the appendix).

✔ **Build positive relationships.** A support network can help you get through tough times.

✔ **Ask for help when you need it.** No-one can be strong all the time. It's important to recognise when you need help.

3.2   Work–life balance

Working at sea can be exciting. It can give you the chance to travel around the world and meet new people.

However, it can be hard to achieve a work–life balance when you live in your workplace.

Work–life balance refers to how you divide your time between work and your social life.

It can be difficult to fit in everything you'd like to when you're working shifts.

You might also find that some parts of work (eg emergency drills) take time from your break periods.

Tips for achieving a work–life balance

✔ **Involve your family in your decision to work.** Make sure you're all comfortable with how long you'll be away and how often you'll be in contact.

✔ **Communicate regularly with friends and family.** Make sure you're open and honest about how you feel.

✔ **Be adaptable.** Accept that things will always change and be ready for the unexpected.

✔ **Plan time with family in advance**, whether this is a port visit or a video call. If you must miss a meeting, make sure they understand why.

✔ **Make sure you have a strong support network at home and/or at work.**

✔ **Separate your work and social life.** Try to switch off mentally from work during rest periods.

3.3   Boredom

Everyone feels bored at some point.

Boredom is unpleasant. It can make you angry, restless or frustrated, and it can make it difficult to concentrate or focus on your job. Boredom can also make you take risks, just to feel some excitement. This can put the safety of everyone onboard at risk.

Boredom is usually caused by having more energy than your task is using up. You might also feel bored when your motivation to do something is low.

Tips to overcome boredom

✔ **Ask for more work or work that will challenge you a bit more.**

✔ **Meditate or practise mindfulness** to help you focus. See section A.2 of the appendix for more information.

✔ **Listen to music.**

✔ **Make a list of activities you can do onboard.** Invite your crewmates to do some of these with you. Activities can be more fun when you do them together.

✔ **Talk to your crewmates.**

✔ **Accept being bored.** It's only a temporary phase, so don't overthink it.

3.4   Smoking, alcohol and drugs

3.4.1   Smoking

Some vessels have a dedicated smoking area.

Smoking causes around 13,000 deaths per day around the world. This is because cigarettes contain lots of chemicals (see Figure 3.1) that cause damage to the body (see Figure 3.2).

Second-hand smoke (inhaling cigarette smoke from the air around you) can also cause damage, so you should try to smoke in a well-ventilated area or away from non-smokers.

Always check with people before you smoke around them, and avoid smoking around children or pregnant women. Don't smoke if you're pregnant yourself: it can cause miscarriage and stillbirth. It can also lead to birth defects (where part of the body is missing or not formed properly).

In some countries, smoking in public places is banned. Check where you can smoke before you travel.

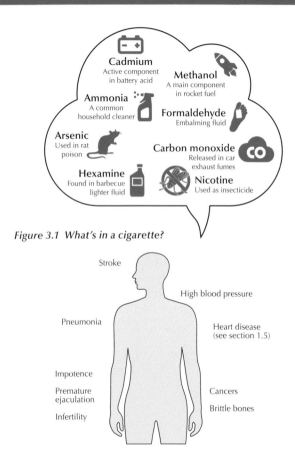

Figure 3.1 What's in a cigarette?

Figure 3.2 Effects of smoking

Cutting down or quitting smoking

Nicotine in cigarettes is very addictive, so it can be hard to quit smoking.

Ways to quit smoking

✔ **Willpower**. You might find it easier to stop smoking if you replace your craving for a cigarette with an activity that takes your mind off it.

✔ **Nicotine replacement treatment**. There are many products that you can replace cigarettes with, such as lozenges, gums and nasal sprays. These give you a dose of nicotine, so you don't crave cigarettes. Most pharmacies will carry them.

3.4.2   Alcohol

Before drinking any alcohol, make sure you're familiar with your vessel's code of conduct and alcohol policy, including the minimum age for drinking, so that you don't break any rules.

You shouldn't drink alcohol while on duty or just before you go on duty.

Alcohol is a chemical found in beer, wine and spirits. The amount of alcohol in a drink is measured in 'units'. Figure 3.3 shows what one unit looks like. One unit is the same as 10 ml of pure alcohol.

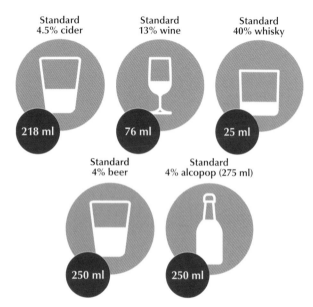

Figure 3.3 One unit of alcoholic drink

In small amounts, alcohol can make you feel more relaxed and sociable, but also less alert and less coordinated. Long-term or heavy use can have many dangerous consequences.

You should never mix alcohol with other drugs. This can put you in much more danger than using drugs or alcohol alone.

You should also never use alcohol if you're feeling low, because it can make you feel worse.

Alcohol is illegal in some countries. Before you travel, make sure you check the alcohol laws in your destination by checking a government website or official travel website.

In countries where alcohol is legal, there is usually a minimum legal drinking age – which might be higher than it is in the UK. It's illegal to buy or possess alcoholic beverages if you're underage.

Alcohol can make you feel overconfident, reckless and uninhibited. It affects your ability to make good decisions and can slow down your reactions. If you drink while you're on duty, you'll be putting yourself and your crewmates at significant risk.

You can see some of the long-term effects of heavy alcohol use in Figure 3.4.

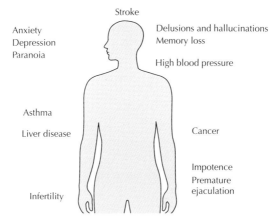

Figure 3.4 Long-term effects of alcohol abuse

If you drink more than 12 units of alcohol a day, you're at risk of alcohol poisoning. Alcohol poisoning can lead to death.

Generally, you should not drink more than 14 units of alcohol a week.

To cut down how much alcohol you drink, follow the tips below.

Read section 3.4.4 if you suspect that you, or another crew member, may be addicted to alcohol.

Check: do you have a drinking problem?

If any of these apply to you, you may have a problem with alcohol. Try to cut down. Ask a doctor for help if you need it.

☐ I drink alcohol every day or most days.

☐ I rely on alcohol to help me cope.

☐ I've tried to quit drinking but it's too hard.

☐ I crave alcohol when I don't drink it.

☐ I've messed up with work or in my personal life because of my drinking.

☐ I put myself in dangerous situations when I drink.

☐ I have to drink a lot to get drunk.

☐ I think about drinking alcohol a lot.

☐ I look forward to drinking alcohol.

Tips for reducing alcohol use

✔ **Set a limit.** Before you drink, set a limit on how much you're allowed to drink, and stick to it. Try to have a few drink-free days each week.

✔ **Choose lower-strength drinks.** You can either swap your normal drink for a lower-strength or alcohol-free version, or you can dilute your normal drink with water or soft drinks.

✔ **Alternate alcohol with water or soft drinks.** Keep yourself hydrated.

✔ **Have a smaller drink.** Cut down on the size of your drink.

✔ **Set personal challenges.** Try setting yourself a challenge of having weekly drink-free days or a drink-free month (eg Dry January).

✔ **Download an app.** There are many useful apps that can help you to cut down on drinking. Look for one that works for you.

3.4.3   Drugs

Your vessel will have a drugs policy and a code of conduct. These will tell you what behaviour is and is not acceptable onboard and in port.

You should not use, sell or give crewmates drugs.

Punishment for possessing or supplying illegal drugs can range from prison to a death sentence, depending on the country you're in. You should check the laws of the country before you travel.

Illegal drugs

Illegal drugs tend to be banned or restricted internationally. You can see examples in Table 3.1.

These drugs have many harmful effects on the body, and can stay in your system for days or even months. So, you might fail a drug test even if you haven't taken anything on the day of the test.

The more you use drugs, the more dependent you can become on them. This means that you'll need more each time to give you the same high as before.

Illegal drugs are often 'cut' (mixed) with other damaging substances, so that the dealer can make more money by selling you less of the drug itself. For example, paracetamol, laxatives and even concrete are sometimes used to add weight to cocaine.

Generally, drugs make you feel overconfident, reckless and uninhibited. Drug use can affect your ability to make good decisions. If you use drugs while you're on duty, you'll be putting yourself and your crewmates at significant risk. You can see some of the dangers of using illegal drugs in Table 3.1.

Table 3.1 Negative effects of illegal drugs

Drug	How long it stays in the body	Negative effects	
		Mental	Physical
Cannabis (weed, hash, skunk, grass, marijuana)	2–3 days (1 joint)	Paranoia Hallucinations or delusions Mood swings Disturbed sleep Mental illness	Lung cancer Infertility Disturbed sleep Increased heart rate and blood pressure
Amphetamine (speed, powder)	1–5 days	Agitation Panic attacks Hallucinations or delusions Mental illness	Heart disease High blood pressure More colds, flu and sore throats Restlessness Comedown: fatigue, depression Heart failure Damage to blood vessels (if injected)

Table continues on next page

Table 3.1 Negative effects of illegal drugs, continued

Drug	How long it stays in the body	Negative effects	
		Mental	Physical
Cocaine (coke, blow, crack, snow)	12 hours to 4 days	Mental illness Panic attacks Paranoia	Nasal damage (snorting cocaine) Damage to blood vessels (if injected) Breathing problems (if smoked) Weight loss Heart attack Seizure
Crystal methamphetamine (crystal meth, crystal, glass)	1–4 days	Mental illness	Dental damage Skin sores Major organ damage
MDMA (ecstasy, molly)	1–4 days	Memory problems Mental illness	More colds, flu and sore throats Seizures Heart attacks Overheating/dehydration

Drug	How long it stays in the body	Negative effects	
		Mental	Physical
GHB (club drug, date-rape drug)	Up to 24 hours	Loss of consciousness Confusion Disorientation	Coma Death Burns to throat and mouth
LSD (acid)	1–3 days	Mental illness Panic attacks Flashbacks Hallucinations	Heart failure Weight loss
Magic mushrooms (shrooms, boomers)	Up to 8 hours	Flashbacks Hallucinations	Nausea Diarrhoea

For more information, you can download the guide to drug abuse at sea by the Shipowner's Club:

https://www.shipownersclub.com/lossprevention/drug-abuse-at-sea/

Prescription drugs

Long-term misuse of prescription drugs can cause lasting health problems too. See Table 3.2 for some of the negative effects.

Table 3.2 Negative effects of prescription drug misuse

Drug	Negative effects
• Anabolic steroids	• Infertility • Erectile dysfunction • Prostate cancer • Heart disease • Organ failure • Manic behaviour • Hallucinations • Paranoia • Mood swings • Aggression
• Diazepam (used to treat seizures and anxiety)	• Drowsiness • Nausea • Low blood pressure • Incontinence • Mood swings • Anxiety • Problems with sleep • Hallucinations
• Morphine (used to treat pain)	• Dizziness • Low blood pressure • Difficulty breathing • Stomach aches/cramps • Loss of consciousness • Coma and death

You should never take any medication that has been prescribed for someone else.

When you're prescribed medication, make sure you follow your doctor's instructions. **Don't take medication if you don't really need it.**

You should inform the medical provider onboard if you're taking any prescription medicines. You should also be aware that some prescription medicines are illegal in other countries. Check with the company whether you can take your medications onboard and in the ports you'll visit.

To learn more about addiction, read section 3.4.4.

Legal highs

'Legal' highs are substances that copy the effects of illegal drugs. They try to avoid the law by making the drug chemically different from the illegal drug that it copies.

The term 'legal' doesn't mean that these drugs have been approved for sale. It simply means that they exploit a gap in the existing drug laws.

Legal highs are dangerous. They're often untested before they're sold, meaning that no-one is sure what the effects will be. Many people have died from using legal highs.

You should be aware that many countries are changing their laws to make these drugs illegal.

3.4.4   Addiction

If you use alcohol or drugs regularly, you should make sure that you have drug/alcohol-free days or weeks. Otherwise, you might become addicted.

Being addicted to or dependent on alcohol or drugs means that you can't function normally without using them.

If you use alcohol/drugs, you might get withdrawal symptoms when you go some time without them. These symptoms include nausea, shaking, excessive sweating, mood swings and sleep problems.

If you feel that you might have a problem with alcohol or drugs, you should speak to a medical professional immediately.

Don't try to stop suddenly. This might cause withdrawal symptoms and can sometimes lead to death. Instead, you might need to slowly take less and less until you can cope with taking nothing.

Check: are you addicted to alcohol/drugs?

Any of these can indicate an addiction:

☐   I don't feel like myself unless I use alcohol/drugs.

☐   I feel like I must use drugs/alcohol despite the risks.

☐   I feel terrible, mentally and physically, when I don't use alcohol or drugs for a while (eg shaking, sweating, mood swings).

☐   I have financial problems.

☐   I isolate myself and push people away.

☐   I need more drugs/alcohol each time to get the feeling I want.

Be vigilant!

It can be hard to speak up if you're worried about a colleague. You may feel it's not your place to say or do anything. You might feel awkward and afraid of getting your colleague in trouble.

It's important for you to remember that if your colleague is suffering with an addiction, they're putting themselves and others at serious risk during work.

It's not always easy to spot addiction in a colleague. You might never see them use drugs/alcohol. But here are some signs that they might need help:

✔ They take a lot of sick leave, with no explanation for their illness.
✔ They have frequent mood swings.
✔ They disappear for long periods, often not explaining where they went or providing a weak excuse.
✔ They seem confused and forget things often.
✔ They make a lot of mistakes at work.
✔ They don't seem to be taking care of their appearance or personal hygiene.

3.5   Overwork

Overwork doesn't necessarily mean that you're working longer hours than you should. It can also mean that you're working too hard or spending more time thinking about work than relaxing.

On a vessel, it can be hard to switch off from work, because you're living in your workplace. Even though your hours of work are controlled by legislation, training and drills can legally cut into your hours of rest.

People who overwork are more likely to use alcohol and drugs, overeat, exercise less, develop heart disease, feel lonely, suffer fatigue and feel stressed.

By overworking, you're putting your health and the safety of everyone onboard at risk.

Check: are you overworking?

Any one of the following, combined with the feeling that you have too much work, may indicate that you're working too hard. This can lead to burnout if you're not careful.

- ☐ I have trouble falling asleep or staying asleep.
- ☐ I have trouble waking up early.
- ☐ I feel stressed.
- ☐ I feel fatigued.
- ☐ I feel lonely or isolated.
- ☐ I'm irritable.
- ☐ I don't perform as well as I used to.
- ☐ I can't focus.

Tips for managing overwork

✔ **Prioritise your daily tasks.**

✔ **Know when to stop.** Don't let work take over your rest or leisure periods.

✔ **Eat well.** See section 1.1.

✔ **Exercise.** See section 1.8.

✔ **Know when to ask for help.** Speak to your supervisor if you feel that you're putting people at risk.

3.6   Stress

Stress is our response to everyday pressures. Anything can cause stress – even positive events in our lives (pregnancy, marriage, holidays, etc.).

Everyone feels stress from time to time: it's a normal reaction to change.

Stress can be useful in situations where we need to be alert (eg during watchkeeping duties).

It's unhealthy when the amount of stress we feel outweighs our ability to cope.

How we cope with stress depends on lots of different factors, such as our personality, health, the availability of support from other people, and how we make sense of the stressful situation or event.

Table 3.3 lists some common physical and mental symptoms of stress.

Table 3.3 Symptoms of stress

In your body	In your mind
• Weight gain • Tiredness • Less energy • Feeling sick • Breathlessness • Frequently needing to urinate • Noticeably stronger heartbeat • Tingling sensations • Less care in appearance/ hygiene	• Negative thoughts • Forgetfulness • Mood swings • Difficulty focusing • Avoiding people • Irritable

Tips for dealing with stress

✔ **Exercise**. It can help to release tension.

✔ **Take slower, deeper breaths**. This can help to calm you down.

✔ **Practise relaxation techniques**. See section A.2 of the appendix.

✔ **Talk to someone about how you feel**.

Check: are you stressed?

If any one of these feelings persists, it may mean that you're stressed out. Follow the tips below to help manage your stress levels.

- ☐ I feel overwhelmed or unable to cope.
- ☐ I feel like I don't have much control in my life.
- ☐ I have trouble falling or staying asleep.
- ☐ I'm irritable.
- ☐ I have more than one of the symptoms of stress (see Table 3.3).
- ☐ I'm going through a lot of changes in my life.
- ☐ I'm under a lot of pressure.

Be vigilant!

Being stressed out for a long period of time can lead to many serious mental and physical health conditions.

If you notice that a colleague is showing signs of stress, speak to them. See how you can help. Sometimes, just being there to listen to them is enough.

If you notice that a lot of your crewmates are stressed, try to get to the bottom of the problem. Think about speaking to your supervisor together or arranging fun activities onboard and onshore.

3.7   Anxiety

Normally, anxiety is a temporary condition in which our bodies prepare for danger.

As a seafarer, you may work in an environment that poses many dangers.

Our bodies react to danger by preparing us to physically fight back (fight), run away (flight) or do neither (freeze). This is called the 'fight, flight or freeze' response.

The fight, flight or freeze response causes a few changes to happen in our body, so that we have the best chance of saving ourselves. You can see these in Figure 3.5.

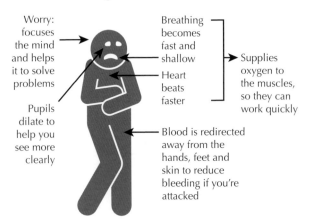

Worry: focuses the mind and helps it to solve problems

Pupils dilate to help you see more clearly

Breathing becomes fast and shallow

Heart beats faster

Supplies oxygen to the muscles, so they can work quickly

Blood is redirected away from the hands, feet and skin to reduce bleeding if you're attacked

Figure 3.5 The fight, flight or freeze response

Sometimes, this response starts happening frequently, set off by things in our everyday life that shouldn't imply any danger. This is an anxiety disorder.

3.7.1   Generalised anxiety disorder

Your risk of developing generalised anxiety disorder (GAD) is influenced by a number of factors, as shown in Figure 3.6.

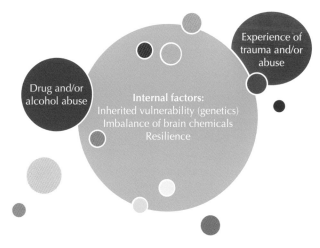

Figure 3.6 Risk factors for developing GAD

The number of symptoms, and their severity, can vary from person to person. Table 3.4 lists the symptoms in your body and in your mind.

You should ask for medical help if you feel that your anxiety is getting in the way of your everyday life: stopping you from working, seeing/talking to people, doing normal things, etc.

Table 3.4 Symptoms of generalised anxiety disorder

In your body	In your mind
• Dizziness	• Feeling on edge
• Tiredness	• Irritability
• Feeling sick	• Uncontrollable worry
• Shaking	• Difficulty relaxing
• Sweating excessively	• Restlessness
• Noticeably stronger, faster or irregular heartbeat	• Feeling like something bad is going to happen
• Tingling sensations	• Feeling afraid
• Stomach, muscle and head aches	• Difficulty concentrating
• Shortness of breath	• Isolating yourself
• Problems with sleep	

Treatment for GAD

There are many effective psychological and medical treatments for GAD. You should speak to a trained medical professional to explore your options.

There are also a few things you can do yourself that might help to manage some of the symptoms. You can see these in the box below.

Self-care tips to manage GAD

✔ **Exercise.** Exercising is a great way to distract your mind. It also releases 'feel-good' hormones that can improve your mood. See section 1.8.

✔ **Eat a balanced diet.** Sharp increases and dips in your energy level can affect your mood. See section 1.1.

✔ **Try to get enough sleep.** Sleep improves your mood and gives you the energy to face your day. You may find some of the tips in section 1.6 useful.

✔ **Try breathing exercises.** These can help to calm your body down if you feel panicked. See section A.2 of the appendix.

✔ **Allocate some time each day to focus on your anxiety.** With GAD, your worries can feel overwhelming and it might feel like something bad will happen if you stop thinking about them. Knowing that you've allocated some time to focus specifically on your worries each day might help you focus more on other tasks that you have to do when you have to do them.

✔ **Challenge your worry.** Write your worries down. Are these worries useful? How do they make you feel? What can you do to overcome them?

✔ **Talk to someone.** Having a support network can really help you deal with and recover from anxiety.

3.7.2   Post-traumatic stress disorder

At sea or at home, you might be exposed to an event that's extremely upsetting, where you feel physically, mentally or emotionally threatened. This can cause post-traumatic stress disorder (PTSD).

Events that can cause PTSD include:

- Witnessing or being involved in a serious accident or natural disaster
- Being attacked, taken hostage or sexually assaulted/raped
- Being diagnosed with a life-limiting illness
- The death of a loved one
- Hearing about a traumatic event that affected a loved one (PTSD by proxy).

If you or one of your crewmates has been involved in one of these events, or something similar, look out for the symptoms of PTSD (see Table 3.5).

Treatment for PTSD

The most effective treatments for PTSD tend to be medical or psychological. The symptoms might sometimes go away on their own with time, but you shouldn't let this put you off getting help. If you're suffering from PTSD, talk to a medical professional.

Table 3.5 Symptoms of post-traumatic stress disorder

In your body	In your mind
• Dizziness	• Reliving the event or feeling like it's happening again through flashbacks and/or nightmares
• Feeling sick	• Avoiding things/people that remind you of the event
• Shaking	• Feeling numb or far away from everything
• Sweating excessively	• Being constantly alert and easily alarmed
• Noticeably stronger, faster or irregular heartbeat	• Difficulty relaxing
• Physical pain	• Mood swings
• Problems with sleep	• Difficulty focusing

Self-care tips to manage PTSD

✔ **Focus on breathing normally.** You might have stopped breathing or stopped breathing normally. This can increase panic, so try to get your breathing under control.

✔ **Keep a flashback diary.** Write down when and where the flashback occurs, and some other details about the experience. This might help you spot patterns, so you can avoid similar situations.

✔ **Carry something that reminds you of the present or makes you feel safe.** This can be useful for bringing you back to the present during a flashback.

✔ **Focus on your wellbeing.** Do things that comfort or soothe you and make you feel safe. This might include listening to music or lying in bed.

3.7.3   Panic disorder

If you frequently have sudden and intense feelings of panic or fear for no clear reason, then you may have a panic disorder.

During a panic attack, you'll have a sudden rush of mental and physical symptoms (see Table 3.6). The experience is usually very frightening or distressing.

Table 3.6 Symptoms of panic attacks

In your body	In your mind
• Dizziness • Feeling sick • Shaking • Sweating excessively • Noticeably stronger, faster or irregular heartbeat • Shortness of breath • Feeling too hot or too cold • Feeling like you can't breathe • Numbness/pins and needles • Dry mouth • Ringing in your ears	• Feeling very scared • Feeling like something bad is going to happen • Feeling detached from your body • Feeling like you're losing control • Feeling like you're going to die

Panic attacks typically last 5–20 minutes. Occasionally they may last longer.

How often you have a panic attack will depend on how serious your panic disorder is.

Panic attacks don't usually cause any physical harm.

Treatment for panic disorder

There are many effective psychological and medical treatments for panic disorder.

If you think that you might be suffering from a panic disorder, you should see a trained medical professional as soon as you're able to.

Sometimes, other conditions (eg low blood pressure) can cause the symptoms of a panic disorder.

Make sure that you're looking after your wellbeing as much as possible to rule out any other causes.

Self-care tips to manage panic disorder

✔ **Exercise regularly.** This will help release stress and tension. Activities such as yoga can be particularly stress-relieving.

✔ **Maintain a healthy lifestyle.** Avoid sugary food and drink, caffeine, drugs, alcohol and cigarettes. Stimulants can intensify panic attacks.

✔ **Practise relaxation techniques.** See section A.2 of the appendix.

Self-care tips to manage a panic attack

✔ **Calm your breathing.** Breathe in and out slowly and deeply.

✔ **Try to focus on good or relaxing images.** You could look at pictures of your family/friends or anything else that makes you feel happy or calm. You can also try touching something soft or comforting.

✔ **Don't fight the panic attack.** Don't do anything reckless to try to stop the attack happening. It's better to let it happen and remind yourself that it will be over soon.

✔ **Remember that a panic attack isn't going to cause you any physical harm.**

3.8   Depression

Depression can be thought of as an disorder that affects your mood, making you feel extremely low and/or suicidal.

Depression is a common health issue, affecting about 3 in every 100 people. Figure 3.7 shows the risk factors that make depression more likely.

Being onboard can be an isolating experience. You might feel lonely or feel you have no-one you can talk to. This can intensify the symptoms of depression.

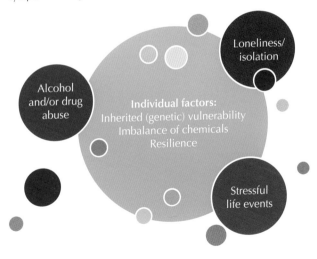

Figure 3.7 Risk factors for developing depression

3.8.1   Symptoms of depression

Table 3.7 lists some common symptoms of depression. The number of symptoms you have, and their severity, can vary from person to person.

If you feel that your low mood is getting in the way of your life, then seek medical help.

Table 3.7 Symptoms of depression

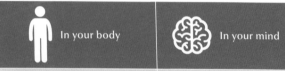

In your body	In your mind
• Changes in appetite or weight (undereating or overeating) • No energy • Moving or speaking more slowly than normal • Low/no sex drive • Sleeping too much or too little	• No motivation • Feeling down and worthless • Negative thoughts • Restlessness • Thoughts about harming yourself or ending your life • Poor concentration • Low self-esteem • Feeling hopeless or helpless

Be vigilant!

It can be hard for crew members suffering from depression to find the motivation to get help. They might not even realise that something is wrong.

Being away from family and friends is hard for a lot of people. If a crewmate seems to be struggling or becomes withdrawn, try to speak to them and see if you can help.

Look out for the symptoms of depression in your crewmates, because sometimes depression can lead to suicide (see section 3.9).

3.8.2   Treatment for depression

There are many effective psychological and medical treatments for depression. You should speak to a trained medical professional to explore your options.

Self-care tips to manage low mood

✔ **Create a healthy routine and try to stick to it.** Try not to let your mood determine what you do.

✔ **Exercise.** Exercising is a great way to distract your mind. It also releases 'feel-good' hormones that can improve your mood.

✔ **Maintain a good level of hygiene.** Small things you do to care for yourself can make a big difference to your mood.

✔ **Challenge negative thoughts.** Write your thoughts down. Are these thoughts useful? How do they make you feel? What can you do to overcome them?

✔ **Talk to someone.** Having a support network can really help you deal with and recover from depression.

✔ **Think about the positive things in your life, no matter how small.** Every day, spend time reflecting on things that went well and things that make you happy. This can help to improve your mood over time. See section A.1 of the appendix for some prompts.

3.9   Self-harm and suicide

Sometimes people can feel so low and helpless that they harm themselves or end their own life.

3.9.1   Self-harm

Self-harm is when you hurt yourself as a way of dealing with difficult feelings, situations or memories.

Anyone is capable of self-harm. It isn't easy to spot someone who does this.

Self-harm includes actions such as getting into fights with the purpose of getting hurt, drinking alcohol or using drugs excessively, overeating, undereating and exercising excessively, as well as more direct ways of hurting yourself (eg cutting).

It's important to understand that you can become reliant on self-harm as a way of dealing with difficult feelings, emotions and thoughts.

If you self-harm, you should seek help. There are many treatment options available.

Self-care tips to avoid self-harm

✔ **Identify your triggers.** Triggers are things that make you want to hurt yourself. They can be thoughts, emotions, memories, people, places, etc. Write down what happened before you self-harmed, including how you felt mentally and physically, to see if there are any patterns. This will help you avoid triggers or distract yourself when they happen.

✔ **Identify distractions.** Once you become aware of a trigger, try to distract yourself until the urge to self-harm becomes manageable or passes. You need to find techniques that work for you. They could include things like reading, watching TV, exercising, spending time with people, etc.

✔ **Delay self-harm if possible.** If you can't overcome the urge to self-harm, try putting it off as long as you possibly can. This will help you gradually build up the gaps between episodes of self-harm until you can stop.

3.9.2   Suicide

Suicide is the intentional ending of your own life. The risk factors are shown in Figure 3.8.

Figure 3.8 Risk factors for attempting suicide

Check: are you/is a crewmate suicidal?

You should be concerned if you notice any of these warning signs in yourself or a colleague:

- [ ] Any of the symptoms of depression described in section 3.8
- [ ] Not thinking or speaking about the future
- [ ] Self-harming
- [ ] Talking about how you/they would commit suicide
- [ ] Stopping doing things that were important to you/them before
- [ ] Giving away personal belongings or planning who should get them
- [ ] Focusing on or obsessing about death
- [ ] Isolating yourself/themselves
- [ ] Taking risks or acting with little concern for your/their life.

What to do if you feel suicidal

- **Phone a helpline.** You can find helpful numbers in section A.5 of the appendix.
- **Talk to someone you trust or a medical professional.**
- **Focus on getting through today.**
- **Don't use drugs or alcohol.**
- **Don't be alone.** Take yourself to a place with other people.
- **Do something distracting that you usually enjoy:** spend time with a friend, watch a film, read a book, etc.

What to do if a colleague is feeling suicidal

- **Don't leave them alone. Alert radio medical services and anyone else who could help**, including senior members of staff.

- **Be supportive**. Don't judge your colleague for feeling suicidal. Just listen to what they have to say and try to keep them safe.

- **Develop a plan of action.**
  - Ask for help and take it in turns to watch the person.
  - **Remove anything they could use to harm themselves**: belts, razors, medication, etc.
  - **Remove anything stressful from their surroundings**: unhelpful people, reminders of loss, etc.

- **Stay with the person until medical help arrives.** You may have to take turns with crewmates to look after the person if you're far from shore.

3.10   Spiritual wellbeing

Spirituality and faith are sets of beliefs that can help people make sense of the world around them. These beliefs usually concern the purpose and meaning of life.

Spirituality is sometimes associated with religion, but it doesn't have to be. You can be spiritual without following a religion.

As a seafarer, you'll interact with individuals with different beliefs and faiths. It's important that you respect others and that they respect you.

The right to express, follow or practise any religious or non-religious belief is part of your human rights.

You shouldn't be discriminated against because of your beliefs. You also shouldn't discriminate against others based on their beliefs. Read section 2.4 to learn about discrimination.

It can be hard to maintain your spiritual wellbeing if being onboard stops you from doing things that you'd normally do: praying, doing something charitable, meditating, etc.

It's important that you dedicate some time to your spiritual wellbeing, as it can have a big impact on your mental and emotional wellbeing.

Your vessel may have provisions to help you with your spirituality or faith. For example, there may be a prayer room onboard, or the master may arrange visits from a chaplain in port.

If your vessel doesn't have such provisions, speak to your manager. Explain any religious or spiritual needs that you may have (eg needing to pray at specific times, or having certain dietary restrictions) and see if anything can be done to help you manage them.

Tips for improving your spiritual wellbeing

- **Make sure you take the essentials for prayer or spirituality onboard with you**: prayer mat, bible, rosary beads, healing crystals, prayer books, meditation aids, etc.

- **Set time aside each day to pray or meditate**. If you need help with either of these, there are many apps that can help you to meditate or pray, depending on your needs.

- **Try learning new things**. Your mind is like any muscle: it needs to be used in order to get stronger.

- **Arrange a spiritual or religious visit during shore leave**. Research in advance the area that you'll be visiting and try to fit in a religious or spiritual activity while you're there.

- **Be kind to others**. Kindness can help boost your mood – and the mood of those you help, too.

- **Reflect on the positive things in your life**. Try to live in the present and don't dwell on the past. You'll find some helpful prompts in section A.1 of the appendix.

- **Speak to someone when you need religious or spiritual advice**. You can either speak to someone onboard or use the contacts in section A.5 of the appendix to speak to someone onshore.

Appendix

A.1   Positive reflection

This exercise is about noticing things that improve your mood, no matter how small they are.

Here are a few examples of the questions you can ask yourself. You can think of more if they help you reflect on the things that you appreciate about your life.

- What went well today? Write down some things.
- What activities make you happy? How can you do these onboard?
- Look around you. What do you like most about where you are right now?
- What do you like most about your family and/or friends?
- What do you like most about your life?

A.2   Relaxation techniques

Relaxation is a state in which you're free from any stress or tension.

Achieving relaxation might be hard onboard because you're surrounded by your workplace.

The techniques below can help you find some relief if you feel tense or stressed. They don't require much room or time.

You should read through the exercises before attempting them.

A.2.1   Breathing exercise

- Place one hand on your chest and the other on your stomach, as shown below.
- Take a deep breath in through your nose, making sure your chest feels full and stretched.
- Exhale slowly.
- Repeat this cycle 6–10 times per minute for 5–10 minutes.

A.2.2   Mindfulness exercise

- Start breathing in and out slowly.
- Breathe in for 3 seconds and breathe out for 4. Breathe in through your nose and out through your mouth.
- As you do this, concentrate on your breathing and nothing else.

- It's normal for thoughts to come into your mind. Don't fight them or get caught up in them; just notice them and gently let them go.
- Continue breathing like this for at least 5 minutes. You can do this exercise for as long as you want to.

A.2.3   Body scan

- Find a comfortable position and focus your attention on your breathing. Breathe in steadily through your nostrils, hold your breath for a couple of seconds and then slowly breathe out.
- When you notice that your breathing is calm, focus your attention on your feet. Notice the sensations you can feel in your toes and the soles of your feet. Once you've acknowledged these sensations, turn your attention to your ankles.
- Take several breaths at each focal point. If you notice an area of tension, breathe in slowly and steadily, then relax as you exhale. Don't move on to the next area until the tension or discomfort is gone.
- Follow this procedure up through your legs, abdomen, chest, fingers, hands, arms, neck and face.

A.2.4   Progressive relaxation

- Focus your attention on both of your feet. Squeeze them tightly, hold for 3 seconds, then release and feel your feet relax.
- Next, focus your attention on your legs. Tense all the muscles, again hold for 3 seconds and relax. Notice how relaxed your legs and feet feel.

- Tense your stomach muscles as tightly as you can. Hold again for 3 seconds and relax.

- Continue tensing and relaxing all the muscles in your body, focusing on a different area each time. Finish by tensing all 43 facial muscles: screw up your face tightly, hold and let go.

A.3   Exercises to do onboard

Space can be limited on a vessel, so the exercises in this section are designed to be done anywhere with 2 x 2 metres of empty space.

If your vessel doesn't have a gym, you might be able to find some space to exercise on the deck, in your living quarters or even in the break room/canteen.

Before you exercise in any of these areas, make sure that it's cool and well ventilated. Also make sure that it's okay to exercise there.

Consider bringing a step counter (pedometer) onboard or download a step-counting app on your phone. Set a daily step target and try to beat it. This can be an easy way to add some exercise to your daily routine. Just adding a 30-minute brisk walk around the deck can make a big difference to your health.

The exercises below are for those with little or some experience of exercise.

If you feel more advanced and want to add some equipment to your exercise, you can bring hand weights and resistance bands onboard. Make sure that you know how to incorporate these into your workout before you attempt to use them.

A.3.1   Warming up

Six minutes is the bare minimum for a warm-up; warming up is just as important as strength training. It prepares the body for a workout, prevents injury and increases blood flow to the muscles.

- March on the spot for 3 minutes, swinging your arms while marching, as shown. This will pump blood to your muscles, increase your heartbeat and prepare you for exercise.

- Do knee lifts for 60 seconds: lift your right knee to touch your left hand, then your left knee to touch your right hand, as shown. Continue alternating between them. Keep your body straight and make sure your supporting leg is slightly bent.

- Shoulder rolls: start to march again, and while marching, roll your shoulders forwards five times and then backwards five times. Repeat this exercise twice.

- March on the spot for 1 minute, swinging your arms while marching.

Once you feel adequately warmed up, continue with the following exercises. You can spend as much time on the exercises as you want, depending on your ability and the time you have available.

A.3.2   The plank

This exercise improves core strength. Lie on the floor and get into the plank position:

- Bend your elbows 90 degrees and rest your weight on your forearms, as shown. Make sure your forearms are directly under your shoulders and your feet are shoulder-width apart.

- Keep your torso in the air, making sure your body is straight and your bottom isn't sticking up. Imagine you're a plank, perfectly straight.

- Is your head relaxed? You should be looking at the floor.

- Tighten your stomach and bottom muscles, and hold for about 10 seconds. You'll get used to this in time, so you can gradually increase it to 20, 30, 45 and finally 60 seconds.

If you can't hold this position, try bending your knees and pushing up on your forearms first. Once you can do this for 2 minutes, move on to straightening your legs.

Remember to breathe steadily.

A.3.3 The squat

This works your bottom and leg muscles. When doing this exercise, it's important to lower yourself in a controlled manner.

- Stand with your feet shoulder-width apart. Angle your toes so they're slightly pointed out – imagine them pointing towards 10.00 and 14.00 hours, as shown (left).
- Bend your knees and push your bottom back and down. Imagine you're going to sit in a chair. Keep your heels firmly on the ground and your back straight, as shown (right).
- Breathe out as you lower your body.
- You can reach out in front of you with your arms for balance.

A.3.4   Push-ups/press-ups

This exercise works your chest and arm muscles.

- Lie on the floor and get into the plank position, as shown (left).
- Make sure your palms are placed directly under your shoulders and your feet are shoulder-width apart.
- Push up your torso and keep it in the air, making sure your body is straight and your bottom isn't sticking up. Imagine you're a plank, perfectly straight, as shown below (right).

- Is your head relaxed? You should be looking at the floor.
- Bend your elbows and lower your chest to the floor.
- Repeat this exercise.

- If you can't hold this position, then try bending your knees, as shown below (left) and pushing up on your forearms first, as shown below (right). Once you can do this for 2 minutes, move on to straightening your legs.
- Remember to breathe steadily.

A.3.5 March in one place

This exercise can be used as a cardio workout.

- Start in the standing position – feet together and hands either relaxed by your side or on your hips.
- Bend your arms at the elbows, to a 90-degree position.
- Lift your left knee to the same height as your hips.
- Lower that knee and lift your right knee.
- Breathe steadily and increase the rhythm.
- Pump your arms backwards and forwards.
- The intensity of this exercise can be increased by marching faster.

A.3.6   The mountain climber

This is a low-impact core exercise.

- Get into the push-up position, make sure your palms are directly under your shoulders and your feet are shoulder-width apart.
- Your body should be as straight as a plank.
- Keep your elbows locked: this will help to stabilise you during the exercise.
- Raise one knee towards your chest, as shown below (left).
- Switch sides without any pause, as shown below (right).
- Breathe steadily.
- Your arms and shoulders should be stable throughout this movement.

A.3.7   The double crunch

This exercises your upper and lower abdominal muscles.

- Lie on the floor on your back. You may find this more comfortable if you have a soft mat to lie on, rather than a hard floor.
- Put your hands behind your head.
- Keep your feet on the floor and bend your knees, as shown (left).

- Curl your body by lifting your head and shoulders off the floor and, at the same time, lift your knees towards your chest, as shown below (right).
- Breathe out as you return to the starting position, and then repeat.
- Don't strain your neck. Your abdominal muscles should be doing all the work.

A.3.8 The reverse lunge

This exercises your legs, glutes and abdominal muscles.

- Begin in a standing position, with your feet shoulder-width apart and your hands on your hips. You should be looking forward, with your chest up, as shown (left).

- Take a step backwards with one foot. Take a deep breath in and lower your back knee towards the ground, but don't let it touch the ground. It should be at a 90-degree angle and should stop about an inch from the floor, as shown (right).
- Your front knee shouldn't pass your toes. Adjust your position by taking a wider step backwards if needed.
- Breathe out as you push yourself up and return to the standing position.
- Swap sides and repeat the exercise. Keep switching sides each time you're in the standing position.

A.3.9   Cooling down

This is as important as the warm-up exercise. It helps your body recover faster and helps return the body to a pre-exercise state.

You can do each exercise for as long as you want, but make sure that your total cool-down is at least 5 minutes long.

March in one spot

- March in one spot, at a slower pace than in your warm-up.

Quad stretch

- You can hold
  onto a wall
  or chair for
  balance if you
  need to, but
  you shouldn't
  put any weight
  on it.
- Stand up, grab
  the top of your
  left foot and
  bend your knee,
  so that your knee points down, as shown (left).
- Bring your foot towards your glutes.
- Repeat with the other leg, as shown (right).

Hamstring stretch

- Lie on your back.
- Lift and straighten
  your leg, so
  that you make a
  90-degree angle.
- Holding your calf
  or thigh, press
  your heel up and
  pull your leg towards your chest, as shown.
- Repeat with the other leg.

Core/back stretch

- Get on all fours.
- Curl up, as shown above (left) then straighten your back slowly, as shown above (right).
- Repeat for 30 seconds.

Chest stretch

- Standing up, interlace your fingers behind your back.
- Straighten your arms away from you, pulling your shoulders back, as shown.

Triceps stretch

- Bend your right elbow, so that your hand is behind your head.
- Use your left arm to gently push the elbow down until you feel a stretch, as shown below.
- Repeat on the other side.

A.4 Checking your body for illnesses

You should be familiar with the way your body looks and feels. It can help you spot when things aren't quite right.

This is especially important for seafarers, as you might not have regular contact with a doctor while you're at sea.

If you find something that concerns you, go to see a doctor. If you're onboard, this might mean waiting until you're onshore.

Once you see a doctor, they should be able to advise on the next steps, if any.

Early detection of illness or disease means more treatment options.

Remember: all your health information is confidential (private). Doctors shouldn't disclose anything without your permission, unless they believe you might be putting yourself or others at risk.

Approach self-examination in the same way you approach other aspects of your health, such as dental health and personal hygiene: build it into your regular routine and report any changes.

A.4.1 Skin

Frequent exposure to sunlight increases the risk of developing skin cancer.

Smoking, drinking and a poor diet can increase the chances of developing other types of cancer (lung, stomach, mouth, etc.).

How do I check for skin cancer?

Remove all your clothing and check your face, neck, torso, arms (including armpits), hands (including fingers), groin, buttocks, and down to your feet and toes.

Skin cancers tend to develop in the places that are most exposed to sunlight (face, head, arms, etc.).

You may find it useful to make notes about large freckles, moles and birthmarks, etc., so that you're aware of any changes.

What changes should I look for?

• Note any changes in the size, shape, texture and colour of moles or birthmarks.

• Note any new moles that have appeared.

• Pay attention to spots or sores that are itchy, hurt, become crusty, scab or bleed, and haven't healed within 3 weeks.

• Note any skin growths that appear pearly, tan, brown, black, multi-coloured or translucent.

If you notice any of these changes, or you have concerns about a mole, freckle or birthmark, speak to a medical professional immediately.

A.4.2   Breasts

Breast cancer can occur at any age. It mainly affects women. (It's also seen in men, but this is uncommon.)

When should I examine myself for signs of breast cancer?

The best time to examine your breasts is approximately 7 days after menstruation.

How should I examine my breasts?

Breast examination ideally should be performed while lying down. Use three fingers (index, middle and ring fingers) to feel for lumps, skin tenderness, thickening or a change in skin texture. Use a circular motion and check the whole breast. Check from your collarbone and armpit, as well as the top of your abdomen.

It's important to apply light pressure at first, then medium and finally firm pressure.

What should I look for?

Stand up and look in the mirror. Do you notice any changes in your breasts or nipples? Lift your arms and check for changes such as:

• Asymmetry
• Redness
• Enlargement of pores
• Dimpling of skin
• Changes in the size or shape of your breasts.

Notice any changes in the nipple: has it changed position, has it become inverted (pushed inward instead of outward) or is there any discharge coming out of it?

If you spot any changes, speak to a medical professional immediately.

A.4.3   Testicles

Testicular cancer can occur in men at any age. However, it's more typically diagnosed in men between 25 and 49 years of age.

When should I examine myself for testicular cancer?

The best time to examine the scrotum is when it's relaxed – for example, during a shower or just afterwards.

How should I examine my testicles?

Check each testicle by rolling it between your thumb and finger.

What should I look for?

- Hard lumps
- Rounded bumps
- An enlarged or heavier-than-usual testicle
- A shrinking testicle
- Pain in the testicle or a dull ache in the lower abdomen or groin.

During self-examination, you'll notice that you can feel blood vessels and the tubes that carry sperm. If you have any concerns, speak to a medical professional.

A.4.4   Urine

What should I look for?

Healthy urine should be a pale yellow to gold colour, and it should be odourless. It shouldn't be frothy or foamy, and it shouldn't hurt to pass. If it's difficult to see the colour of your urine, just check that it isn't frothy/foamy and that it doesn't smell.

Any changes to this could reflect your diet, how much water you drink, or illnesses such as urinary tract infections, diabetes, kidney disease or cancer.

If your urine is consistently different from this, even after changing your diet or drinking more water, then speak to a medical professional.

If you spot blood in your urine (unless you're menstruating), speak to a medical professional.

A.4.5   Bowel health

What should I look for?

Healthy stool (poo) is medium to dark brown in colour and soft to firm in texture. It will smell strongly. You should normally pass stool at least three times a week, and it shouldn't hurt to pass.

Any changes to this could reflect your diet, how much water you drink, or possibly an illness.

If your stool is consistently different from this for 3 weeks (eg too hard to pass or too loose), even after changing your diet or drinking more water, then speak to a medical professional.

If you spot blood in your stool, speak to a medical professional as soon as possible.

A.4.6   Coughs

Coughs can be a normal part of minor illnesses and tend to go away on their own. You may also have a persistent cough if you smoke (known as smoker's cough). Although a smoker's cough isn't always a sign of illness, you should try to cut down how much you smoke (see section 3.4).

Sometimes, a persistent cough can be a sign of something more serious, such as a viral infection, asthma or lung disease.

What should I look for?

You should be able to get over-the-counter medication from pharmacies or supermarkets to treat your cough. You should seek medical advice if:

*   You have a cough for more than 3 weeks
*   You find that you're bringing up greenish-yellow phlegm
*   You're wheezing
*   You have chest pains or get short of breath when you cough
*   You're coughing up blood.

A.4.7   Hands and nails

Hands and nails are useful indicators of general health. They can reveal if you have conditions such as iron deficiency, high blood pressure, high cholesterol and arthritis.

You put your hands through a lot, especially when doing manual work. Make sure you take care of them: wash them regularly with gentle soap, dry them well, and moisturise them so they don't split and crack. You should try to avoid products containing many chemicals and perfumes, as they can damage your skin and cause allergic reactions.

What should I look for?

You should seek medical advice if any of the following are present persistently (over 3 weeks) when examining your hands and nails:

- Discolouration in your nails that can't be explained by anything else (eg staining with food or bruising your nails)
- Split or cracked nails or hands, despite using moisturiser
- Red blotches on your hands
- Very pale hands and nails
- Swelling around the knuckles and joints
- Shaky hands
- Pins and needles or numbness in your hands.

Remember: you use your hands frequently, so it's normal for them to get worn, calloused, bruised or damaged. These indicators are just a guide, so be sensible. You should only be concerned if you can't think of any logical reason why your hands or nails have changed. It's always best to check with a medical professional if you're unsure.

A.5   Useful contacts

Apostleship of the Sea: port chaplains and ship visitors who offer wellbeing advice and support for seafarers regardless of faith or religion.

Website: **https://www.apostleshipofthesea.org.uk**

Befrienders Worldwide: emotional support to prevent suicide. Helpline available on the website.

Website: **https://www.befrienders.org**

Big White Wall: free online therapy and support for a range of wellbeing issues.

Website: **https://www.bigwhitewall.com**

The Fishermen's Mission: provides emergency support and practical support and advice for a range of wellbeing issues. For active and retired fishing crew and their families.

Website: **http://www.fishermensmission.org.uk**

FRANK: honest information about drugs.

Website: **https://www.talktofrank.com**

ISWAN SeafarerHelp: free and confidential, multilingual helpline available 24 hours a day for seafarers and their families, whatever their problem, wherever they are in the world

Phone: **+44 20 7323 2737** (free callback)

Email: **help@seafarerhelp.org**

Website: **https://seafarerhelp.org**

ITF (International Transport Workers' Federation): advice about working rights and justice.

Website: **https://www.itfseafarers.org**

MIND: information and advice about mental health and wellbeing.

Website: **https://www.mind.org.uk**

Mission to Seafarers: Provides a range of care and support including ship visiting, seafarer centres, free wi-fi, transportation, counselling and spiritual care.

Website: **https://www.missiontoseafarers.org/help-where-can-i-get-help**

NHS: advice and information on a wide range of health and wellbeing issues.

Website: **https://www.nhs.uk**

SAIL (Seafarers' Advice and Information Line): free, confidential advice about benefits, debt, employment, housing, pensions, relationships, immigration and more. Based in the UK.

Phone: **0800 160 1842**

Website: **http://sailine.org.uk/how-we-help**

Sailors' Society crisis response network: trauma care and counselling service for crises at sea.

Website: **https://www.sailors-society.org/ourprojects/crisis**

Seafarers Hospital Society: charity dedicated to helping seafarers with health and welfare. Services include free physiotherapy for all working seafarers and priority medical treatment. Based in the UK.

Website: **https://seahospital.org.uk**

Seafarer Support: directory that can signpost you to charities and welfare organisations to help with your issue.

Phone: **0800 121 4765**

Website: **http://www.seafarersupport.org**

SeaWives: support for partners of seafarers.
Website: **http://www.seawives.com**

Index

Bold page numbers indicate figures, *italic* numbers indicate tables.

abandonment by shipowner,
    repatriation after 100–102
abortion 55, *55*, 56
addiction 124–125
age of consent 50
alcohol 113–117, **114**, **115**, 124–125
allergies *8*, 8–9
amphetamines *119*
anabolic steroids *122*
anxiety **130**, 130–133, **131**, *132*
Apostleship of the Sea 169
assault 83–84
    sexual assault 84–88

back stretch exercise 162
balanced diet 1, **4**
Befrienders Worldwide 170
beliefs, spiritual 146–148
Big White Wall 170
blood pressure 21
body, checking for illnesses
    163–169
body language 50, 51, 63, 64, **65**
body mass index 6
body scan 151
bone and muscle injuries/disorders
    34–36, **35**
boredom 110

bowel health, self-examination for
    166–167
breasts, self-examination of
    164–165
breathing exercise 150
budgets, managing personal 91–94
bullying 75, 76, 78, 79

calories 1
    see also diet
cannabis *119*
carbohydrates 2
    see also diet
catfishing 105
chest stretch exercise 162
cigarettes, content of **112**
climate conditions, management of
    heat exhaustion 29, 30
    hypothermia **31**, 31–33
    sun *27*, 27–29
clothing 16
cocaine *120*
communication
    body language 50, 51, 63, 64, **65**
    conflict and 65–66
    cultural differences 68–71,
        69–70
    effective 63–64
    importance of 63

communication *continued*
    teamwork and 65–66
    verbal/non-verbal 64, **64**
condoms *53*
conflict, communication and
    65–66
consent for sex 49–52
contraception 52, *53–55*, 55
core/back stretch exercise 162
coughs
    self-examination for 168
    spread of infection, preventing
        17
crime
    assault 83–84
    criminalisation 88–89
    defending self against charges
        88–89
    law and 79–80
    piracy 81–83
    responsibility for 79
    sexual assault 84–88
    theft 80–81
criminalisation 88–89
crystal methamphetamine *120*
cultural differences 68–71, *69–70*
cyber bullying 105
cybersecurity
    fake news 104
    internet connection 102
    phishing emails 104
    safety online 103
    scam emails 104
    social media 104–106

dairy foods *2*
    see also diet
dehydration 10–13, **11**
depression 139–142, *140*
diazepam *122*
diet
    allergies *8*, 8–9
    balanced 1, **4**
    body mass index 6
    calories 1
    carbohydrates 2
    controlling 1
    dairy *2*
    fats *3*
    fruit *2*
    improving 7
    intolerances 9–10
    musculoskeletal disorders
        (MSDs), avoiding 36
    nutrients 1
    proportions of foods *2–3*
    proteins *2*
    special 7
    vegetables 2
    vitamins 1
    weight, under/over, risks of 3, **5**
discrimination 75, 77–78
double crunch exercise 158–159
drugs
    addiction 124–125
    illegal 117–118, *119–121*, 121
    legal highs 123
    policy/code of conduct 117

possessing/supplying illegal 117
prescription 121, *122*, 123

ecstasy *120*
emails 104
emergency contraception tablets
    55
emergency IUDs *55*
emotional wellbeing
    addiction 124–125
    alcohol 113–117, **114**, **115**,
        124–125
    anxiety **130**, 130–133, **131**, *132*
    boredom 110
    depression 139–142, *140*
    drugs 117–125, *119–121*, *122*
    generalised anxiety disorder
        130, 131–133
    overwork 125–127
    panic disorder 136–138, *137*
    post-traumatic stress disorder
        (PTSD) 134–136, *135*
    resilience 107–108
    self-harm 142–143
    smoking 111–113, **112**
    spiritual wellbeing 146–148
    stress 127–129, *128*
    suicide **144**, 144–146
    work-life balance 109
employment rights for maternity/
    paternity 58–60
exercise
    back stretch 162
    benefits of 33

chest stretch 162
cooling down 160–162
core/back stretch 162
double crunch 158–159
equipment 152
hamstring stretch 161
marching 157, 160
mountain climber 158
MSDs and 36
onboard 151
plank, the 154–155
push ups/press ups 156–157
quad stretch 161
reverse lunge 159–160
space for 152
squats 155–156
step counters 151
tips for 34
triceps stretch 162
warming up 153–154

faith, spiritual 146–148
fake news 104, 105
fatigue 23–25
fats *3*
    see also diet
femidoms *54*
fight, flight or freeze response **130**,
    130–131
finances, managing personal 91–94
Fisherman's Mission 170
fitness 33–34, 36
    see also exercise

food *see* diet
FRANK 170
fraud 105
fruit 2

generalised anxiety disorder **130**,
      131–133
gestures, cultural differences and
      68, *69–70*, 71
GHB *121*

hamstring stretch exercise 161
hand-arm vibration 37–38, **38**
hands, self-examination of 168–169
harassment 75, 77–78
heart/heart disease **22**, 22–23
heat exhaustion 29, 30
heat stroke 29–30, **30**
hydration 10–13, **11**
hygiene, personal 15–20
hypothermia **31**, 31–33

illegal drugs 117, *119–121*, 121
illnesses, checking body for
      163–169
infectious diseases 40–42
International Transport Workers'
      Federation (ITF) 170
internet
   connections 102
   safety online 103
   scam emails 104
   useful websites 169–171

intolerances, food 9–10
intra-uterine devices (IUDs) *54, 55*
isolation 72
ISWAN Seafarer Help 170
ITF (International Transport
      Workers' Federation) 170

legal highs 123
LGBTQIA+ community 45
loneliness 72–73
LSD *121*

magic mushrooms *121*
malware 105
manual handling procedures 36
marching exercise 157, 160
marijuana *119*
maternity-related employment rights
      58–60
MDMA *120*
mental and emotional wellbeing
   addiction 124–125
   alcohol 113–117, **114**, **115**,
      124–125
   anxiety **130**, 130–133, **131**, *132*
   boredom 110
   depression 139–142, *140*
   drugs 117–125, *119–121*, 122
   generalised anxiety disorder
      130, 131–133
   overwork 125–127
   panic disorder 136–138, *137*
   post-traumatic stress disorder
      (PTSD) 134–136, *135*

resilience 107–108
self-harm 142–143
smoking 111–113, **112**
spiritual wellbeing 146–148
stress 127–129, *128*
suicide **144**, 144–146
work-life balance 109
MIND 170
mindfulness exercise 150–151
Mission to Seafarers 171
money, managing personal 91–94
morning after pill *55*
morphine *122*
motion sickness 13–15
mountain climber exercise 158
musculoskeletal disorders (MSDs)
34–36, **35**

nails, self-examination of 168–169
NHS website 171
nicotine replacement treatment 113
noise 39–40
non-verbal communication 50, 51,
63, 64, **64**
nutrients 1
see also diet

online safety 103
over/underweight, risks of 3, **5**
overwork 125–127

panic disorder 136–138, *137*
passports 45
paternity-related employment rights
58–60
personal hygiene 15–20
phishing emails 104
piracy 81–83
plank, the, exercise 154–155
positive reflection 149
post-traumatic stress disorder
(PTSD) 134–136, *135*
pregnancy
avoiding 52–56, *53–54, 55*
managing onboard 58–61
separation from pregnant
partners 61
prescription drugs 121, *122,* 123
press ups 156–157
privacy 74
progressive relaxation 151–152
proportions of foods *2–3*
proteins 2
see also diet
PTSD *see* post-traumatic stress
disorder (PTSD)
push ups 156–157

quad stretch exercise 161

rape 84–88
statutory 50

relationships
    abortion 55, *55, 56*
    consent for sex 49–52
    contraception 52, *53–55,* 55
    good sexual health 58
    long-distance 46–47
    pregnancy, avoiding 52–56,
        53–54, 55
    pregnancy, managing onboard
        58–61
    romantic, with crewmate 47
    sex 49–52
    sexually transmitted diseases
        56–57
relaxation techniques 149–152
religious beliefs 146–148
repatriation 100–102
resilience, personal 107–108
reverse lunge exercise 159–160

safety
    online 103
    onshore personal 84
SAIL (Seafarers' Advice and
    Information Line) 171
Sailors' Society 171
scams 104, 105
Seafarer Support 171
Seafarers' Advice and Information
    Line (SAIL) 171
Seafarers' Hospital Society 171
seasickness 13–15
SeaWives 171

self-examination for illnesses
        163–169
self-harm 142–143
sex
    abortion 55, *55, 56*
    consent 49–52
    contraception 52, *53–55,* 55
    good sexual health 58
    pregnancy, avoiding 52–56,
        53–54, 55
    sexually transmitted diseases
        56–57
sexual assault 84–88
sexuality 42–46
sexually transmitted diseases 56–57
skin, self-examination of 163–164
sleep 26
smoking 111–113, **112**
sneezing and coughing 17
special diets 7
spiritual wellbeing 146–148
squats 155–156
statutory rape 50
step counters 151
steroids *122*
stress 127–129, *128*
    post-traumatic stress disorder
        134–136, *135*
stretching exercises 161–162
suicide **144**, 144–146
sun, staying safe in the *27*, 27–29

teamwork
  communication and 65–66
  conflict and 65–66
teeth brushing and flossing 16,
    19, **20**
testicles, self-examination of 166
theft 80–81
tiredness 23–24
travel, safe 94–100
travel sickness 13–15
triceps stretch exercise 162
trolling 105

ultraviolet (UV) radiation 27
under/overweight, risks of 3, **5**
urine, self-examination of 166–167

vegetables 2
  see also diet
verbal/non-verbal communication
    64, **64**
vibration 36–38, **37**, **38**
vitamins 1
  see also diet

warming up for exercise 153–154
washing 16, 17–18
water, drinking 10–13, **11**
websites, useful 169–171
weight, under/over, risks of 3, **5**
wellbeing, importance and meaning
    of xiv
whistle-blowing 89–90
whole-body vibration 37, **37**
work-life balance 109